I AM A
CARD COUNTER

I AM A CARD COUNTER

Inside the World of Advantage-Play Blackjack!

Frank Scoblete

TRIUMPH
BOOKS

Library of Congress Cataloging-in-Publication Data

Scoblete, Frank.
    I am a card counter : inside the world of advantage-play blackjack! / Frank Scoblete.
        pages cm
    ISBN 978-1-60078-947-2
    1. Blackjack (Game) I. Title.
    GV1295.B55S365 2014
    795.4′23—dc23   2013042590

This book is available in quantity at special discounts for your group or organization. For further information, contact:
        Triumph Books LLC
        814 North Franklin Street
        Chicago, Illinois 60610
        (312) 337-0747
        www.triumphbooks.com

Printed in U.S.A.

ISBN: 978-1-60078-947-2

Design by Sue Knopf

For my teammate and wife,
the beautiful AP

Contents

Introduction:
Yes, I Am a Card Counter

I have a dual personality for this book and for my next one, *I Am a Dice Controller*. Originally I was going to combine these two games and my experiences playing them into one book. As the first draft of that book progressed, I realized that the length would have been equivalent of the entirety of Wikipedia. My publisher (unfortunately) does not pay me by the word, and I also didn't think the publisher would want to pay for all that binding material and the herd of elephants needed to cart the books from bookstore to bookstore, country to country, across the Alps, and to the mysterious underground warehouses the Internet sellers maintain wherever they maintain them.

So I decided to split that massive book into two different ones—one focusing on my playing career in blackjack and one focusing on my playing career in craps. You might say these two books take place in parallel universes. If you have the ability to take each universe and press them together, you get it all. I hate to say this, but even I can't do that. Although it will look as if I lived two advantage-playing lives, it was just one—a fun one, an interesting one, sometimes a harrowing one.

While I was going great guns at blackjack with my wife and partner, the beautiful AP, during the 1990s and early 2000s, I was learning to become a competent, then good, then (no humility here) great dice controller. The path to being a great dice controller (or even a decent one) requires hard work and a significant investment of time. It took me quite a bit of time.

I was at the top of my skills in blackjack as we went into the 21st century, but my skill at dice control was competent but marginal. As the 21st century began, I found my way in dice control, and my skill soared just in time to see the slow decline of excellent blackjack games. One door opened while another almost closed.

Although this book will focus on blackjack, I was playing craps during this time as well. I might refer to the craps play where I think it will be necessary for readers' comprehension or easier to digest it all. It is certainly going to be easier for me to write about all of it.

Of course, this book is not just about me—a topic I love and of which I can't seem to get enough—it is also about some of the greatest blackjack players in the world, living and deceased. Blackjack advantage play has a long history, from the mid-1950s through today. It is a history filled with interesting characters, great players, and wild stories…many of them actually true.

I know many readers are looking for tales about the millionaire advantage players, and some of those players *are* in this book. But winning millions is not always the sign that a player is great. Ted Williams, in a 23-year baseball career, played in only one World Series, and he was arguably the greatest hitter who ever lived. His teams just didn't have what it took to go all the way. Some blackjack players, while great, also don't have what it takes to bet large sums of money. Movies won't be made about them. Nor will they be the subjects of books. They will remain unknown to all but the few who know just how great they are.

The best blackjack player I ever met was a small-stakes player. You'll find out why. This guy taught me more about blackjack than any book I ever read. He was the greatest in my estimation, and in the estimation of many terrific players who knew him. Most other players—even those who have won millions—cannot match this man's skill, or even come close. The man had everything—except enough money to play big and the permission of the Las Vegas casinos to play at all. Being *allowed* to play is just as important as how well you play.

I have some connection to most of the players I write about in this book. I've seen them play firsthand—which, to me, is important—and I've developed friendships with some of them. Some of these players are in some way connected to me through others I've written about. Some are simply my standard of what it means to beat the casinos. Some are simply great writers who have given me strategies and insights.

Why aren't all great players (who are allowed to play) million-dollar winners? Some can't bring themselves to see money as merely chips. At a certain point they just can't put a $500 or $1,000 or higher bet out there. That type of money makes them blanch. They have an absolute sense of the value of a dollar and the value of thousands of dollars, and the emotional cost of losing such sums is just too high. It rattles them. Other advantage players have no such hesitation. To them chips are just chips.

"Chips are just chips" is the best philosophy to have as an advantage player, but for most players it is extremely hard to think of money in non-absolute terms. If you bet $10, and that $10 is 10 percent of your $100 bankroll, that amount will not usually cause you to sweat uncontrollably or feel your heart pound in your chest. But make that a $10,000 bet against a $100,000 bankroll, and it seems to be a far bigger percentage, even though it obviously isn't.

Some of the advantage players in this book are examples of what can be done if one really tries to beat the house. They might not actually enter the realm of the "greatest," but they are still inspiring people. There are card counters all over America, and they are playing right now as you read this book. There are even some players who can follow cards in a shoe, figure out when those cards should come into play, and then bet accordingly. There are players who can catch the dealer's hole card and take advantage of that knowledge. Despite the fact that blackjack games have deteriorated throughout the country, there are still opportunities to take it to the house.

In addition to discussing some of the best blackjack players ever to play the game, *I Am a Card Counter* is also a highly personal book for me, as it relates the adventures I had with the beautiful AP, and with many of my friends and teammates. *I Am a Card Counter* is about players I knew and enjoyed knowing—and players I knew but didn't enjoy knowing. Some of these players are just like your average man or woman next door, just as AP and I appear to be your typical suburban couple; some of these players are characters of a different stripe, meaning they are really, *really* characters. Some have passed away, and others are still out there playing the game. For all you know, the next time you sit down at a blackjack table, you may be sitting next to one of them.

Blackjack represented a way of life for my wife and me; we played as a team for more than a decade. Even after my wife retired from the game and the casino life, I continued to play the game—and have done so for more than a quarter century.

I have lived those 25-plus years in a world remarkably different from the world most of my non-advantage-play contemporaries lived in—both those who played casino games and those who never set foot inside a casino. It was a world of adventure and skullduggery, bright sunshine and horrible rains, fear and laughing and loathing. It was a world where I learned what the casino industry was really all about and a world where my one goal was to extract the golden tooth from the casino dragon's slobbering mouth and take the damn thing back home with me.

I hope you enjoy this book, because I enjoyed the quarter century of adventures that created it. It's been some ride!

CHAPTER 1

In the Beginning

I was part owner in a theater company on Long Island, New York, from 1979 to 1990. It was called the Other Vic Theatre Company, in honor of the Old Vic Theatre in England. By the way, you never say "I live *in* Long Island" the way you would say "in New York" or "in Cleveland" or "in Las Vegas." For some reason you live "on" Long Island. And Long Island is exactly what it sounds like—a *long* island, going from Brooklyn and Queens, which are two boroughs of New York City, all the way to Montauk Point, which is at the very eastern tip. Usually when folks refer to "the Island," they forget about anything to do with New York City and just consider it two counties, Nassau and Suffolk. I live in Nassau.

The theater company was thriving. We toured various libraries, charitable organizations, and dinner theaters and we also had our own 500-seat permanent theater. My partner in the company was a smart and interesting woman—a teacher by day and a producer, director, and actress by night (with matinees on weekends). We had a good partnership.

In the late 1980s I decided to produce *The Only Game in Town* by Frank Gilroy, a brilliant play that (go figure) only ran for a couple weeks on Broadway. My co-star was Alene Paone, who had been working with us as a stage manager for about three years. Alene was a lithe, good-looking, effervescent 29-year-old woman—a perfect fit for the role of Fran Walker, a Vegas chorus girl throwing her love away on a rich businessman using her for the usual reasons a rich businessman uses a woman. Rich businessmen make great villains, don't they?

I played degenerate gambler Joe Grady, a craps player who wished for luck on every roll of the dice but rarely had any. He did have an electric personality, but he was a short circuit as a human being. He was down and out. He was looking—hoping—for one big score so he could leave Vegas and start a normal life. It did not look as if that score would ever come. He was—to make this short but not sweet—a loser in life and a loser in love.

Joe and Fran meet, they fall in love, and after some dramatic ups and downs, the play ends happily with Joe making the big score at craps and an even bigger score with Fran. And the businessman gets screwed—figuratively. As I said, a very happy ending.

The problem we had with the play was a problem we had with ourselves: we knew nothing. When it came to casino gambling, we had no idea what we were saying. Alene knew about the idea of being a chorus girl: you danced and maybe sang some songs as a backup to a star. But she had no idea of what I was saying when I discussed the game of craps, though onstage she had to look as if she was totally cognizant of what everything meant. I had these great monologues that can really stretch an actor and rivet an audience, but what the hell was I actually saying? I had never played craps; I knew nothing about the game. Indeed, I had never played any casino games, nor had Alene. Blackjack was news to me, although I did know what roulette consisted of—I had seen scenes involving roulette wheels in movies, and, of course, James Bond made a fortune betting on number 17. In college I had played poker, but that was it as far as gambling went.

Alene and I decided we'd go to Atlantic City and learn craps and watch it being played. Alene, even at 29 in an age after the sexual revolution (the revolution that gave men the wonderful license to have sex without worrying about having to marry the woman—nothing like "getting the milk and not having to deal with the cow," as my late grandmother scornfully said), insisted on having her own room. After all, I was a married man with two young sons. I don't know if she knew how much I actually did love her; in fact from the very moment I met her, I loved her, but that's a tale I told in my book *The Virgin Kiss*.

We stayed at the Claridge, a small casino in a beautiful old-world building. It was also the building in which I was conceived, which proves the saying, "What goes around comes around"...or maybe, "You can go home again." At the Claridge I was lucky to meet up with the man who would ultimately become my gambling mentor, "the Captain" of craps, along with his crew of 22 high rollers. He taught me the game, and when I performed my role as Joe Grady, I knew exactly what I was talking about.

I also knew that casino gambling offered me a new life, because I was becoming disenchanted with theater, disappointed with my relationship with my partner, and disenchanted with my life, my wife, and my future—in short, I was a kind of Joe Grady, the very character I had played, looking to get out.

I did stay with the Other Vic Theatre Company for another year or so, during which time I did one of the best plays ever written, my own *Dracula's Blind Date*, certainly strong competition for Shakespeare's best plays. During that time I studied casino games. I wanted to know if it was possible to actually beat them.

When I had been in the Claridge, I watched a few blackjack games and wondered, *If no aces are left in the shoe, no one can get a blackjack. Is there a way to follow the cards to get an edge at the game?* I thought this was a profound insight on my part, not knowing that far greater minds than mine had figured out just about all the ins and outs of the game far better than I ever could. They had discovered something called "card counting" that allowed a player to follow the cards and bet more when the edge in the game favored him and less when the game favored the casino.

Most casino games are stagnant. The casino's edge is the same from decision to decision, and there is no way a player can change that. However, with blackjack the play of the cards changes what will come up in the following hands. If there are no aces left in the deck, there will be no blackjacks. A player can wish, pray, and hope, but if those aces are gone, those blackjacks are gone. Card counters can exploit this knowledge of what remains to be played.

Most casino games couldn't be beaten—at least not by average people like me. But blackjack and craps were different. Blackjack could be beaten with card counting, and the Captain was showing me that craps could be beaten with dice control. During my time with the Captain and his crew, I got to see the Captain roll, and I also got to see the greatest dice controller of all time, a woman known as "the Arm."

The difference between card counting and dice control is the difference between night and day. Blackjack probabilities change with the play of each hand; what cards have been played determines what cards will be coming up. If the decks favor the player, the decks will favor all the players, whether those players know it or not. In craps, the probabilities do not change unless a controlled shooter can change them with his skill. The shooter determines whether the game favors him, not the play of the cards or the play of random shooters who compose the overwhelming majority of craps players. The shooter dictates the nature of the game.

While I toured in *Dracula's Blind Date* during my last days of working in theater, I studied the game of blackjack. Unlike craps, I did not have a personal mentor. I went it alone and studied constantly.

I bought many books, such as *Beat the Dealer* by Edward O. Thorp (the first real card-counting book ever written); *The Theory of Blackjack* by Peter Griffin (filled with math and also fun stories); *The Big Player* by Ken Uston and Roger Rapoport (a knockout book with the story of the most famous, flamboyant "big player" of all time, Ken Uston, who has inspired many blackjack players over the decades); *Million Dollar Blackjack* by Ken Uston; *The World's Greatest Blackjack Book* by Lance Humble; *Professional Blackjack* by Stanford Wong (a bible for me, Wong put it all into perspective); *Playing Blackjack as a Business* by Lawrence Revere; *Ken Uston on Blackjack* by Ken Uston; *The Beginner's Guide to Winning Blackjack* by Stanley Roberts; *The Blackjack Formula* by Arnold Snyder (whose magazine *Blackjack Forum* was a must-read in my early career); *Two Books on Blackjack* by Ken Uston; *Blackjack Your Way to Riches* by Richard Canfield; and *Blackjack's Winning Formula* by Jerry L. Patterson.

Some other books not put on this list were basically junk, selling betting systems that could not beat the game. I learned about betting systems when I used a martingale at the Sands casino in Atlantic City. The martingale is a betting scheme where you double your bet after a loss, the philosophy being you have to win sooner or later. True. The problem is that after six to eight losses in a row, doubling your bet after each loss, you usually hit the table limit and are destroyed. I was betting five dollars and doubling after each loss. While successful for two days, each win only won me five dollars. When the axe fell, I lost a lot of money. So much for betting systems.

It was one thing to read about blackjack, but I had to practice card counting to get any good at it. I bought a blackjack shoe (the contraption that holds multiple decks of cards) and practiced a count called the Hi-Lo. In this count, the 2, 3, 4, 5, and 6 are counted as plus-one, and the 10, jack, queen, king, and ace are counted as minus-one. The 7, 8, and 9 are neutral. When the shoe favors the player, meaning the 2s through 6s have come out in sufficient numbers to make the shoe positive (favoring the players), you bet more money; when the 10-valued cards and aces come out, making the shoe negative (favoring the casino), you bet your minimum bet. To be sure, there are many wrinkles in this method. The count has to favor you sufficiently so you really do have an edge and you have to bet enough in these counts to overcome the overall edge the casino has in the game. For example, if you are playing a four-deck shoe and the count is a +8, moving your bet from $10 to $20 is not going to be enough to overcome the overall house edge. If $10 to $20 is the only increase you make in counts that favor the player, you will not win at the game in the long run. In shoe games you also have to establish the "true count" in addition to the "running count"—by dividing how many cards remain into the running count. This "true count" gives your true edge, which is the edge you use for wagering amounts. Positive edge, bet more; negative edge, bet less. Simple idea with a profound impact on playing the game.

Another very important aspect of playing advantage blackjack is making the correct decisions on your hands against the dealer's up-card. This method is the computer-derived "basic strategy." Playing by whim is a poor way to go and probably a losing way, too even if you do count cards. (I doubt there are card counters who play their hands by whim.) Certainly, there are slightly different basic strategies for different games, usually based on the number of decks. But the changes are relatively small and certainly not all that important in four-, six-, and eight-deck games.

In 1990 Alene Paone—forever now known as the beautiful AP—moved in with me. She had her own room in my rented condo; I was not going to let my sons think we lived together as anything other than friends—even though we were much more than that.

I spent every afternoon and many nights playing hands on the dining room table. I dealt myself round after round after round of hands—keeping the running count, converting to the true count, and betting accordingly. I played four-deck games, six-deck games, and even eight-deck games, which were starting to take over Atlantic City. The more decks, the more patience you must have, as the counts change somewhat slowly. The casino generally has a higher edge the more decks a game contains. [There are some exceptions to this; for example, the new single-deck games that only pay 6-to-5 on blackjacks are probably worse than just about any multiple-deck games that I played.]

I did learn certain things that served me well. Many advantage blackjack players hold false notions about the game. One has to do with how fast you can count down a deck of cards. You just keep flipping the cards over as fast as you can to see if you can count down the deck properly. Some blackjack teams actually use this as a test of how good a card counter is.

At first I thought this was important, and I would practice counting down a single deck—bam, bam, bam, bam. Then I watched games in the casino and realized that even the fastest of the fastest dealers were actually pretty slow. The key was not to watch the dealer scurrying through his cards but simply to watch the cards on the table. The dealer could not deal like the superhero Flash, and those cards sat on the table for a sufficiently long enough time to have no problem counting them. It was nothing like the bam, bam, bam, bam of counting down a single deck. I learned to simply keep me eyes on the cards and not on the dealer's motions.

Gamblers have myths about play—almost all of which are wrong—but so do advantage players. Belief systems can make you see what you want to see. This is called "confirmation bias." Counting down a single deck in a few seconds does not have any real meaning in a real game. The speed of blackjack games is actually easy to handle. I would say that all blackjack games are relatively slow, even the ones everyone thinks are fast. As I said, don't watch the dealer, just watch the cards.

Once I had a handle on how to play and I knew I was good, I told the beautiful AP, "I want you to learn blackjack. I want us to eventually become a team. I want us to take it to the casinos."

"Okay," she said. And she started learning the Hi-Lo count as well.

The Problems Pile On

Even though AP and I were living together, at that time my financial state was a mess. My then-wife, Lucille, was dragging her feet on our divorce. I had written up what I felt was a fair divorce agreement that we could take to mediation and avoid conflict and unnecessary expense (my lawyer thought I was nuts and said, "You are giving her everything"). She'd get the house, I'd pay for her to go to graduate school to get a degree in library science, I'd pay child support, I'd pay the mortgage until the divorce, and I'd take the kids every weekend. (Yes, I hate to say this, but I even took the kids to Atlantic City and Vegas.) I'd also give her spending money until she could find a job.

While Lucille happily took everything I offered, she wouldn't budge on giving me a divorce. She was a woman who never wanted to work. She hired a radical feminist attorney who wanted all of the stuff I had offered her plus half my pension from teaching plus both of my testicles, nicely roasted, on a sterling silver platter.

I had sold my theater company by that time. My partner had tried to get me to pay off all the company's liabilities while she got all the assets. Our company's lawyer explained to her that any liabilities the company had must be bought along with all its assets. The company was in a great financial position: the liabilities were small, the income was great.

Still, I wanted out, and I took a minimal payment for my half of the company. My partner—my former partner, that is—could have it. I was done with theater, and the prospect of going through endless "negotiations" with her made me essentially walk away.

During that period of time, it seemed that life was done with me. I was a loser, perhaps a worse loser than Joe Grady. Even though I actually wanted to lose some of those things I lost, I was sinking into deep debt.

I remember sitting on the beach at Cape May, New Jersey, a place I have always considered my retreat, with the beautiful AP just before we started our team play. I was morbidly reflecting on my life's situation. (I'm a good morbid reflector.)

I intended to send my kids to Chaminade, a private Catholic high school, perhaps the best on Long Island. I was sending Lucille to graduate school. I couldn't get the damn divorce without a battle in court, meaning lawyers' fees. And I had taken too little for my half of the theater company. I was almost $50,000 in debt at that point (remember this was in the early 1990s), and with the ongoing child-support payments and giving Lucille spending money, I was in quicksand. I was sinking.

Oh yeah, another little (make that *big*) knife plunged into my back during this time: I was told I would lose my teaching job of 16 years at the end of the school year. The superintendent of the Lawrence Public Schools in Cedarhurst, Long Island, was Dr. Alvin Baron, and I had alienated him over the years by being obnoxious (totally *my* fault—as a young man I was too stupid to be cordial to those in authority) and also being a strong union head at the high school when he was principal there for a year before assuming the superintendent's position. I set the framework for this guy to screw me.

Dr. Baron figured out a clever way to screw me, too. He was "excessing" me after 16 years in the English department, which meant that even though I had tenure, I could be let go because I was low man in the department and my job no longer existed. In short, I was excess baggage. Tenure can't save you if there is no job for which to be saved. My teaching career could be over.

But there was one little wrinkle that I could exploit. I could bump someone in the social studies department if I could get the social studies certification in one year, which required 30 credits for a master's degree. There were at least four social studies teachers over whom I had seniority.

When I have to do something, then I do it. I went to graduate school at night, during holidays, and in the summer and got my degree. The guy I bumped out of the social studies department was Dr. Baron's fair-haired boy (actually he had black hair), and as soon as I told the stunned superintendent, "There's no problem, I can now bump into social studies," he suddenly discovered that my English position miraculously reappeared after he had caused me to spend a small fortune trying to save my neck.

So you can see I was really, really down in the dumps sitting on that lovely beach at Cape May. I looked at the ocean—so blue, so peaceful—and I looked at my life—so blue, so full of pieces—and I whined.

The beautiful AP has a can-do attitude, and she "can-doed" me right there as I listed my miseries. "You have nowhere to go but up," she said. "I'm telling you, things are going to work out. You'll see. You'll pay off your debts, you'll get the divorce, your kids will go to Chaminade, you'll even be able to pay for them to go to college without them taking loans. And you'll even become a famous writer."

I had written two plays and many articles for local papers, but I really thought I had no big future as a writer. I was 40 and had achieved very little.

"In what?" I asked. "I don't have any other ideas for plays or anything."

"I don't know," she said. "I just have a feeling. I can tell you this, think of this scene right here on the beach, right here in Cape May, because from right here and right now you go all the way up."

I threw a couple of small stones into the ocean and said, "I hope you're right, my beauty, I hope you're right. I don't know how I'm going to do this."

"You'll do it, you'll see," she said.

The Beautiful AP and King Scobe Unleashed

In the midst of decay, new life can sprout—think of winter into spring—and that is exactly what happened to me. I learned how to count cards, and the beautiful AP and King Scobe (my students used to call me King Scobe or Scobe, and AP calls me Scobe; it's a nickname reserved for those who truly know me) headed for Atlantic City, this time not to watch but to finally play. That first week was great. We spent eight days there, and we won each and every day. I say "we," but AP preferred to watch during that time so she could gain confidence that she could actually count with a casino dealer dealing the cards.

That week was so special I actually conned myself into thinking that if we continued to do that well, we'd wind up owning a casino. I was a small-stakes player, too, going from five dollars on my low hand to $50 on my highest hand—in shoe games your bet spread, low to high, has to be greater than in single- and double-deck games. I recall walking along the Boardwalk trying to figure out which casino I would buy. I would tell AP how we would run our own casino. She just smiled and shook her head. Such was my imagination, such was hubris, such were the seeds of destruction.

We won $5,000 that week, an amazing amount considering how much I was betting. The games we were playing were good, mostly four decks with deep penetration. Penetration, meaning how many cards are cut out of play, can determine whether a game is good or bad. The better the penetration, the better the game. The actual rules of the game are not usually as important as the depth of its penetration.

I was truly a strutting cock of the Boardwalk after that first visit, and then we went back to Atlantic City a few weeks later and I was the cock that got squashed by a car while trying to cross the road. I had put aside $5,000 as a bankroll, and during that first trip we doubled it. The second trip saw me lose every penny of that money—I mean, every penny of our win *and* every penny of my initial bankroll. My final destruction occurred at the Claridge in the high-roller room when I had a bet of $2,500 on the table on various hands that I had split, resplit, and doubled on. I was so convinced that my bad luck had to (*had to!*) change that I was betting way too much for my almost nonexistent bankroll. Succinctly, I was a complete idiot, trying to recover all my money in just a few hands. I was on tilt, I wasn't thinking straight—hell, I wasn't thinking at all. I was the very ploppy player I have made fun of over the years.

At that moment of the "Frank Scoblete is the Titanic about to hit the iceberg," the count was sky high; my hands went from 18 to 20. The dealer was showing a 6. He had to have a 10 in the hole because so many small cards had already been played and I was sure he would bust with his piddling 16 and I would come roaring back and recapture my original 5K stake. From there on, casino ownership had only been delayed by a small losing streak. *Move over, Steve Wynn and Donald Trump, the new boy—Frank Scoblete, card counter—is in town.*

The dealer flipped over his hole card. Oh yeah, a 10! He had 16, just as I thought. My heart was racing with joy; it was racing with excitement. Then something hit me—a small thought in the back of my mind that suddenly came roaring to the front: *I haven't seen many 5s during this shoe*. I started to sweat. I started to really sweat, and everything went in slow motion from that; at least that's how my memory sees it. He pulled out a card from the shoe and slowly flipped it over. A 5! A bead of sweat went down my nose and dropped onto the table. A 5, oh my God, a fucking 5!

I was busted. I had lost every penny I had reserved to play blackjack and start my casino-playing career in order to get myself out of debt. On one flip of the cards I had lost $2,500. In one trip, I had lost $10,000. My gambling stake was gone. My confidence was gone. The casino I was going to buy was gone. I was, at that moment, the ultimate loser.

On the way back to Long Island, the beautiful AP and I stopped at the Captain's house. As soon as he saw us, he smiled and said, "There they are with empty pockets."

I guess he could see it written on our foreheads and in our depressed state. He then proceeded to give me a lesson I have never forgotten—a lesson on bankroll and betting within your bankroll. He discussed the underlying emotions of having an advantage at a game and how those emotions can do you in if you aren't careful. Those emotions had certainly done me in because I wagered a monstrous amount of money against a mini-amount of bankroll on that trip. Emotions will often cancel out thinking; in advantage gambling, emotion is often one of the worst elements in maintaining an edge over the house. The Captain would always tell me, "The struggle is not between you and the casino; it is between you and yourself."

He was right. I lost my bankroll not because I couldn't beat the casinos at blackjack; I lost my bankroll because I couldn't beat back my feelings.

I learned my lesson, too. I never lost another bankroll. I built up a bankroll that would take the "end of days" to lose. I have used the Captain's insights and advice all these years, and they have stood me in good stead. Perhaps it is best to take your beating right off the bat. I once read somewhere that compulsive gamblers often start their gambling obsession with a great win or two the first times they play. This stimulates whatever regions in the brain desire that pleasure again. I didn't have to worry about that.

And to make everything wonderful, I also got the Captain's permission to write a book about him and his ideas—and he wanted no money or even publicity from the deal! I just had to keep his name a secret. That book—*Beat the Craps Out of the Casinos: How to Play Craps and Win!*—launched my career as a gambling writer. Since then I have written or edited some 40 books, some of which are about the Captain's methods of play, the particulars of which I shall write about in *I Am a Dice Controller*.

CHAPTER 2

The Greatest Blackjack Player

"I want to meet the greatest blackjack player in the world," I said to Howard Schwartz, manager of the Gamblers Book Shop in Las Vegas. "If he's not in Las Vegas, just help me get in touch with him. I want to know who he is, and I want to talk to him."

"Want me to change a base metal into gold while I'm at it?" asked Schwartz. That was Howard—quick of wit, highly intelligent, sarcastic, and knowledgeable. If anyone knew the greatest blackjack player in the world, it would be Howard. In the world of gambling, it seemed that Howard Schwartz knew everyone.

This was June of 1991, several months before my first gambling book, *Beat the Craps Out of the Casinos*, was published, and at the time, Howard managed the Gamblers Book Shop for Edna Luckman, the owner. Edna was a classy lady, and you'd be hard-pressed to think she was one of the movers and shakers of the casino world. She seemed more like a kindly grandmother than a tough-minded businesswoman in a world totally controlled by men until relatively recently.

In 1964 Edna and her late husband, John Luckman, created the first bookstore, publishing house, and mail-order business that strictly dealt with gambling. They brilliantly filled a niche for hundreds of thousands of hungry players looking for good information about various gambling games they loved to play.

The Luckmans were legends in the Las Vegas of the 1960s, '70s, and '80s, but when John Luckman passed away, Howard Schwartz took over the reins of the business, though Edna still spent considerable time in the store. She was truly a lovely woman, and she made a giant impact on casino players. She was the Aunt Bee of the casino industry. (Aunt Bee was a beloved character on *The Andy Griffith Show*.)

Her greatest piece of advice to gambling writers: "For most games there isn't too much new you can write about them, so what you have to do is approach these games in a different fashion. You have to have a different voice from the rest of the writers. Do that, and you will be successful."

The sharp-tongued Howard Schwartz was also a legend in Las Vegas and in gambling circles throughout the country. The Gamblers Book Shop and its affiliated mail-order company, the Gamblers Book Club, gave many gamblers what they wanted and in fact needed: books and tapes about how to properly play the games or bet the horses or go into a poker room without fear of being stripped of their dignity and, more important, stripped of their dough. It was an honor to have one of your books in Schwartz's store, and I couldn't wait to see mine on the shelves. This small store was a mecca for gambling writers and players from across the nation, and even the world.

Any visit to the Gamblers Book Shop was an adventure for me. As a novice gambling writer, I was always excited to meet the great gaming personalities who frequented the place. The Gamblers Book Shop was certainly a thriving business, but it was also a modern library and seminar room for gamblers—all the wise ones, the published ones, and even those hopeless ploppies. It was a place where folks could argue theories, discuss math, and analyze which casinos in Vegas were giving players the best deals. High rollers rubbed shoulders with those who were having trouble putting two dimes together. It was a complex compendium of the best, the worst, the brightest, and the dimmest. The Gamblers Book Shop was a must-stop when one went to Vegas.

Howard Schwartz orchestrated the patrons in his store the way a conductor does a symphony. He was a host, a salesman, and a sage, always willing to take time to talk to you. Howard was a true gentleman of the New York variety—which means occasionally tart-tongued, with ample amounts of his tongue set firmly in his cheek.

"Can you get me in touch with the best blackjack player?" I asked again.

"Let me go to my office and see what I can do," he said. "I expect a commission."

"You do know who he is?" I asked.

Howard gave me a look that said, *Of course I know who he is*.

A couple of moments later, a shabbily dressed worker came from the back. He was about 5'7" or so and looked somewhat tired. Howard probably had the guy loading stock in the warehouse section of the business.

"I'm Paul Keen," he said. "Can I help you?"

"I'm just waiting for Howard. He's getting something for me."

Paul smiled. "I'm what he's getting for you."

"Excuse me?"

"Howard said you wanted to meet the best blackjack player in the world," he said. "I really don't know if I am the best in the world, but for many years I made my full living playing blackjack."

Paul Keen? Paul Keen? I never heard of him. *Who the hell was Paul Keen?*

I had heard of Ed Thorp, the founder of the modern system of card counting, whose book *Beat the Dealer* revolutionized the game, or at least revolutionized the game for players who actually wanted to get an edge at the game. I had heard of Ken Uston, known as "the Big Player" (also the title of the exciting book about his exploits as a million-dollar card counter), who was perhaps the most famous and flamboyant blackjack player of all time. I'd heard of Lawrence Revere and Stanford Wong and Henry Tamburin and

Lance Humble and Arnold Snyder. Of course, I wouldn't necessarily know Paul Keen, since he hadn't written a book, but from looking at him I wondered how this guy could be considered the best of the best in the world of blackjack. Shouldn't the best in the world be rich? Shouldn't the best in the world be driving a Rolls-Royce? Shouldn't the best be dressed better? I was dressed better than he was, and I was (and am) a terrible dresser.

I thought Howard Schwartz was having some fun with me. Maybe there was no such thing as the best blackjack player in the world. This guy, this Paul Keen, was a stock boy, for crying out loud. How could he be the best blackjack player in the world?

Keen knew what I was thinking. "You expected someone a little more imposing didn't you?" he asked. "I left my James Bond tuxedo at home. It's hard to load the shelves and package the books in the envelopes, wearing a tuxedo."

Howard came from the back just then. "This man is the greatest blackjack player that I know of," he said, nodding at Keen. "When any of the great names you read about have a question about the game, they come to Paul. Uston used to come around here all the time to talk to him."

"Ken Uston? *The* Ken Uston?" I asked. Ken Uston was a blazing star in the blackjack firmament. Ken Uston and Paul Keen?

"*The* Ken Uston," Howard said.

If Howard said this guy was the best, what the hell. It couldn't hurt to talk to him. Maybe Howard wasn't pulling my leg.

"Okay," I said. "I wanted to pick your brain. I am writing a new book on blackjack, and..."

"Fine, at dinner tonight, a good restaurant, your treat," he said.

If I previously had my doubts about this guy, my doubts doubled. *My treat?* The best blackjack player in the world? *My treat?* Shabbily dressed, somewhat disheveled...*the best in the world?* I guessed it would be worth a dinner at a "good restaurant" to find out the truth. I again wondered if this were some elaborate joke Howard was playing on me.

"Okay, dinner tonight at 7:00. I'll give a call to the store in about an hour and let you know where I've made reservations."

"Where are you staying?" he asked.

"The Maxim," I said. "I just got in about an hour ago and then came right here."

He laughed and said, "Luck is with you. The Maxim has the best blackjack game in the history of Vegas. Check it out when you go back."

"I will," I said.

And that is how I met Paul Keen.

The Maxim casino is no longer around; it closed in 2001. Perhaps it is most noted in the general public's mind as the property outside of which famous rapper Tupac Shakur was gunned down in 1996. The building now houses the Westin.

My wife, the Beautiful AP, and I had selected the Maxim because it was inexpensive and just two blocks from the strip. The place had a coffee shop and a good steakhouse. So the steakhouse it was for our dinner—*my treat*—with Paul Keen, supposedly the greatest blackjack player in the world.

When I got back to my room, I told the beautiful AP about my initial observations of the "world's greatest blackjack player."

"It is weird that the guy would tell you flat-out that you'll treat to dinner, after telling you that he wants us to have dinner with him to begin with," she said. "He creates the dinner date and then creates the fact that we pay for the dinner date."

I called the Gamblers Book Shop and told Paul Keen that we'd meet him at 7:00 PM at the Maxim steakhouse.

"I'll be bringing my girlfriend, Susan," he said, and hung up.

I turned to AP and said, "We're evidently treating his girlfriend, too."

"He might not be the greatest blackjack player in the world," said the beautiful AP, "but he sure knows how to cage a free meal. He's a comp magician."

Paul arrived right at 7:00 PM, with his girlfriend. "This is Susan," he said. "I live in her luxury trailer."

I introduced them to AP, and we went inside to have dinner. The restaurant was not crowded; it only filled up on the weekends, and it was only Wednesday.

As we were seated, Paul said, "Did you check out the blackjack games? The single-deck ones? I think there are four tables."

The Maxim was a small hotel with a small casino. It probably had only 15 to 20 blackjack tables. In 1991 the unbeatable carnival games such as Caribbean Stud, Let It Ride, Three-Card Poker, and such had not yet squeezed their way into the blackjack pits. The casino had two craps tables and a single table in their poker area peopled by weird players. I played poker there on occasion, and it did—at times—seem like a loony bin.

"I didn't check the games," I said. "I went to the room, called you, and fell asleep."

We ordered drinks. "You count cards?" asked Paul.

"Yes," I said. "We both count cards. But this is our first extended trip to Vegas; we'll be here for two weeks. We've been playing four-deck games in Atlantic City."

"Are you any good?" he asked.

"We're good; I guess we're good," I said.

"We're good," said the beautiful AP.

CHAPTER 3

The Beginning of the End-Play

"You'll like the Maxim's single-deck game," Paul said. "It is the best single-deck game ever in Las Vegas. I don't ever remember a game this good, and I've been playing a long time."

"Vegas has great single-deck games," I said. "That's why we flew out here: to play the games and research my new book." That new book would be *Best Blackjack*.

The waiter brought us our drinks. We toasted to a great trip.

"The game uses all but one of the cards, which is discarded after the shuffle. If the dealer runs out of cards midway through the hands, he just takes the discards, shuffles them, and continues dealing."

"God," I said.

"The rules are great, too. Dealer stands on soft 17 [which is an ace-6], you can surrender your hands, and you can double on any two cards and split three times."

"God," I said again.

"And every time you get a blackjack with five dollars or more, you get a one-dollar coupon you can use anywhere in the hotel."

"God," I said yet again.

"And it's actually worth one dollar," he said.

"God, they're giving away the money," I said.

"They're only giving it away to some of us and not all the card counters either. Check out the casino," he said. "This restaurant is almost empty, but the casino is packed with players. The single decks are bringing the players in, but only so many can play the game since there are only four tables. But the other players just feel the urge to play and have to satisfy their urge to play, so they play the six-deck games, which aren't so hot and don't have the best rules. The casino manager of this place is pretty clever. He brings the players in for the best game in town, but most of them play inferior games."

"The crowd gets the adrenaline flowing," I said.

"Exactly," Paul said.

"The craps tables are full," AP said. "The slot machines are being played all over, too. So you think that covers the losses to card counters at those single-deck games?"

"Some card counters are even getting hit at the single-deck games, too," Paul said. "They aren't winning as much as they should be."

Paul's girlfriend, Susan, was reserved. A petite, pretty, intense woman of about 35, she didn't really seem all that interested in talking about blackjack. She really didn't seem all that interested in talking about anything. But Paul enjoyed relating his experiences, and Susan seemed to be a good listener. Susan was a sexy woman, although she wouldn't have met society's definition of a beautiful woman. She had her own unique look. But she had *that* way about her, and *that* way was sexy. *That* way also meant she was sexy without trying. She made no attempt to be sexy. If we really do react to pheromones, then Susan had them in abundance. Obviously Paul loved her, for he was quite solicitous of her during the meal. Still, she really talked very little.

* * *

Paul Keen had started off as a relatively big player, betting green and black chips, but Vegas has never been a friendly town to skilled card counters. The casinos have finely honed radar to catch card counters—it used to be other skilled players hired to catch the counters but now consists of computer systems developed to do the same thing. Even though card counting is perfectly legal (you are allowed to use your mind in a casino, even though most players prefer not to), the casinos have the right to tell you to stop playing and even to tell you never to come back to their properties.

Slowly over the years Paul had been banned from just about every casino. Then something happened: he managed to get some of the pit bosses to allow him to play five-dollar games with his high bet no more than $15. As he said, "They gave me that, at least." Why they did that, I have no idea; Paul must have used some magic formula.

In blackjack card counting, a player bets small when the cards remaining in the deck favor the casino, and in Paul's case, that would be five dollars. A player bets big when the cards remaining to be played favor the player, and in Paul's case that would be $15. The cards favor the casino when more small cards—2, 3, 4, 5, and 6—remain, and the cards favor the player when more 10s, jacks, queens, kings, and aces remain. Paul's bet spread from low ($5) to high ($15) was quite small, but it was sufficient to get him in the advantage game against those great single decks that existed in Vegas during those heady days of the early 1990s.

On a good single-deck game, a bet going from five dollars to $15 was enough to get the card counter a small edge. I'm guessing that Paul probably could expect to make $15 per hour on average. Of course, that average was over time, and in the short run a card counter faced tremendous volatility, meaning wild ups and downs. Some nights you got your ass kicked, some nights you kicked ass, some nights you won a little, and some nights you lost a little—but over time a good counter at those great single-deck games could win money with just a $5 to $15 spread. But you couldn't really win a lot of money unless luck became your lady not just for one night but for the rest of your life. Luck doesn't seem to work like that for most of us.

Paul claimed he spoke to the pit bosses personally, and maybe he begged them to allow him to play for such small stakes. No wonder he lived in a "luxury trailer" owned by his girlfriend and was a salesman/inventory specialist at the Gamblers Book Shop. Vegas was not going to allow Paul Keen to win substantial sums of money, even if some casinos let him play. That's not how Vegas works. Vegas exists to take money *from* people, not give it *to* them. Las Vegas is the anti-charity; it delights in snatching money, not bestowing it. If Vegas were a science fiction movie it would be called *The Invasion of the Money Snatchers*.

Paul certainly had his ups and downs over the years. At times he lived out of his car because he didn't want to use his bankroll to pay for room and board. I thought that unusual at the time I heard it, but over the years I have discovered that many advantage players, especially poker players, have resided in their cars when things went south. I never had to worry about that, as I always had a job to fall back on. And as my writing career became successful, my books and columns allowed me to live a decent life—and to gain weight at a remarkable clip as I enjoyed the eating and imbibing my casino career afforded me.

Thankfully, Howard Schwartz hired Paul and then Susan housed him, so when I met him he at least had a job and shelter. Happily, he was also allowed to play blackjack for small amounts. I guess that was a success, considering he could have had no girlfriend, not been allowed to play in the casinos, and not had a job.

Paul's personal story was interesting, but I am sure there were many people living in luxury trailers whose stories were interesting, too. But I had no interest in those interesting stories. I was interested only in Paul Keen and only if he were really the best card counter in the world, as Howard Schwartz had claimed. He certainly talked a good game, but how did he play? I would see that night.

When we went to the casino after dinner, there were two open spots on one of the single-deck games. Paul took one spot, and I took the other. I had never played that type of single-deck game—all but one card dealt and new deals with the discards when the cards were all played. If the deck ran out and the round wasn't finished, the dealer just took the discards, shuffled them, and continued the play. Although I knew the basic strategy for the games I had been playing in Atlantic City, the new style of play threw me. As I played the game, it just didn't feel right.

"Let's quit," Paul said. He was up about $60. I was down about $20. My spread was $5 to $20. He said, "Let's go to your room." So AP, Susan, Paul, and I took the elevator to our room.

In the room Paul took out a deck of cards and shuffled. He said, "There's a type of play, known as 'end-play,' that almost no one knows nowadays. When all the cards are dealt out but not all the players have received their full hands, those discards now change the nature of the game—they flip your count. Understand?"

"Let me get this," I said. "If the discards contain small cards, the count is high, and normally you'd bet big, but if the cards run out and you haven't gotten your two-card hand, what's about to come out will be small cards."

"Right," he nodded. "So you have to know that if you are betting into a positive count [meaning it favors the players] your big bets won't be ruined because that second card you are getting will most likely be small. So you have to be careful and make sure you know approximately how many cards are left in the dealer's hand so you don't get caught by the reshuffle. Also, if a dealer is showing a small card and has to hit that small card, those discards coming into the game could help him make his hand. Or they can bust him if the discards contain a lot of high cards."

"I never thought of that," I said. "It changes the nature of the game."

AP jumped in. "So many of your average, everyday card counters are actually hurting themselves not knowing this end-play? So this great game can actually hurt them at times?"

"Yes," Paul said. "By giving such a game that has never been played before, the card counter might not be able to handle that reshuffling in the middle of a round of play."

"Jeez," I said. "You put the big bets out, and *bam!*—the cards run out and you are now playing a negative deck when the discards come back into the game. It's so obvious now. I wonder why it didn't occur to me. It works the reverse, too. You can see that you have small cards and the high ones are about to come out. That can change how you play your hands. I can't believe I never thought of this before."

"Don't worry about it," Paul said. "Almost no one knows about end-play because games like this are almost never played, at least in my lifetime. But card counters—most of them, anyway—are creatures of habit and just play by rote. They rarely think to look at a truly unusual game and see if it has some unique pitfalls."

"The reverse is also true," AP said. "I've got it, too. Just as Scobe said, if the count is low but you have no cards or one card, you can expect a great number of high cards in the discards. If you know the cards are going to run out before they get to you, then you put up a big bet."

"The count only seems low at these times, but in fact it is high, often favoring the end-player by a lot," Paul said.

"Man," I said. "Man."

Paul said, "That's end-play. You get the hang of that, and your edge on this game will be the highest you can imagine. Off the top the player has a small edge on this game even if he doesn't count cards but plays basic strategy. You will have the best blackjack game you ever played if you master end-play."

"And the dollar for every blackjack," I said.

"And surrender," said the beautiful AP.

"God," I said.

"Let's have dinner tomorrow night," Paul said.

"Our treat," I laughed.

"Your treat," he said. "And I'll teach the two of you end-play. You've got a great game here, and your two weeks in Vegas should be rewarding."

At that point, there was no doubt in my mind that Paul knew his stuff. End-play? I had never heard of that, and if it were in any of the dozens of books I had read, I must have skipped right over it.

End-play?

Amazing.

Paul Keen?

Amazing as well.

CHAPTER 4

Masters of End-Play

I spent the next day relaxing by the pool after a vigorous workout at the spa at Bally's, the hotel-casino across the street from the Maxim. I figured I'd just get my body used to Vegas—the hot, *hot* Vegas in the summer, with its dry heat, as they say (a heat that can shrivel you into a prune if you don't guzzle gallons of water)—and just wait until I knew how to really take advantage of Maxim's single-deck game.

The next night, after a scrumptious dinner at the steakhouse, Paul, Susan, AP, and I went back to our room. Paul took out a deck and taught us end-play.

As we played, Paul would ask us how many cards were left in the dealer's hand and if he would run out, thereby reshuffling the discards, and how that reshuffling would affect our hands, the dealer's hand, and our betting and strategy decisions. At first AP and I were awful, truly awful. We just could not nail down the number of cards that were in the dealer's hand, and thus we made mistakes that cost us money. Then after about an hour, we started to get close. Then more often than not, we started hitting it just about right. I could see its effects. The game could more often than not just flip around, depending on when the dealer ran out of cards.

"Do the casinos know about end-play?" I asked.

"Most don't. Unless the pit boss or dealer is an old-timer, it's a way of playing that isn't well known. Today's games rarely have a need for it. I actually don't think many card counters know it. Maybe the casino manager who brought the game in knows about it; I'm guessing he does."

At the end of several hours, Paul put the cards down and said, "Let's go down and see if we can give this a try in a real game."

So we went down and gave it a try.

That night turned our blackjack-playing careers around. I became a great end-player (don't expect humility from me), and the Maxim's heaven-sent single-deck game took us from spreading $5 to $20 up to $25 to $200 (there were some occasions where I actually had my bet up to $500).

We extended our trip to eight weeks—we'd have to get back to the East Coast to start the school year after Labor Day—and what made the Maxim so utterly, fabulously great was the fact that the floor people and pit bosses knew we were counting; they knew others were counting and didn't give a damn. It was like playing on your dining room table—no sweat, no heat, nothing to do but keep the count and bet appropriately. For a card counter it was like dying and instantly going to heaven.

The beautiful AP and I then played for those eight weeks, logging in eight hours per day, with each of us playing two hands. When the count was high, we wouldn't really go slowly up the ladder of bets. We'd jump—$25 to $100 to $200. When the count was high we had a minimum of $800 on the layout—four hands of $200—as opposed to $80.

Our end-play helped, and some of the dealers, through boredom or because AP and I were two of the few players who gave them tips, would occasionally show their hole card as they dealt or would do a double take when they had a 4 in the hole to check for a blackjack. This double take was more often than not a real mistake because the edge of the 4-card often looks like the edge of the ace. Nevertheless, that was a signal that they didn't have the ace underneath their 10-valued up-card. In those days, Maxim did not have the card readers that casinos use today to see what the dealer has in the hole.

I really don't know if the dealers were doing any of these "mistakes" on purpose, and obviously I didn't ask. Interestingly enough, in Las Vegas if a dealer makes a mistake that favors you, that mistake is not your problem and you do not have to rectify the situation. Under the law, you are perfectly justified in keeping the money made from the mistake.

AP and I took advantage of every situation that presented itself. By playing four hands for eight hours per day, we accumulated a fortune in $1 coupons, because the average is about one blackjack every 20 hands, so (on average) one of us would get a blackjack every five rounds. Those $1 coupons added up; except for the first couple of nights, we never had to pay for a meal while we stayed there. (The Maxim did not comp us, however, one of the things that showed they knew we were playing with an edge.)

With the best rules ever, with relaxed executives, and with personable dealers, the Maxim game was far and away the best blackjack game I ever played. It took me from being a small-stakes player and started me on my way to being a big, literally fat, high roller.

How could the Maxim afford to allow such games at their four tables? Keen had answered that question correctly: players who showed up played the other games if they couldn't get in on the single-deck games, and hard as this is to believe, many players who played that single-deck game had no idea of how to play blackjack! They had no idea of just what a wonderful game they were sitting at. Basic strategy to them was whatever whim they felt at the time they played their hands. "I think I'll do that; no, I think I'll do this."

Of course, there were many card counters who made their appearances—a few of whom I recognized. Most of them were good players, although some wrote better books than their playing skills warranted. Paul Keen played just about every night after work. I got to see him in action, and even then I knew this guy was truly in his own class. My end-play ability helped me quite a lot, and so did my fearlessness in getting my big bets out when the count called for it. Still I was not Paul Keen. I didn't know how he did it at the time, but he seemed to have an uncanny ability to predict when he was going to get a blackjack. Since he was able to bet more than $15 max in the Maxim single-deck game, he'd jump to $50 in a player-favorable moment, and it was stunning how often those blackjacks came to him. (That $50 was his maximum bet.)

AP and I made some new friends at that Maxim game. There was Ken Rose, a teacher from Maryland who owned multiple properties and horses. He was an excellent player but just couldn't get the really big money on the table when the count called for it. He froze. Money was dear to him.

There was Peter Nathan, a writer and good card counter, who came to Vegas with his son, Michael, to play the Maxim's game. Peter was an expansive kind of guy and made friends easily. He loved to have dinners with gambling celebrities. No dinner with him had fewer than six people; it was as if he were holding court. Then there was Silas, one of the cheapest men I have ever known— and I've known some cheap ones. (Silas is not his real name but a pseudonym in honor of Silas Marner, that great cheapskate character crafted by George Eliot.)

We made a good friend in one of the Maxim's dealers, Nicki Perry, who had a similar background to AP and me. AP and I were involved in theater and then moved on, while Nicki had been a dancer on cruise ships. Still, as inevitably happens, the time came for her to retire and find a new career. She became an excellent dealer, and as AP and I played our daily morning sessions, she was often our dealer. And she was the only dealer who made no "mistakes" in our favor. Indeed, as our time at the Maxim made the place our second home, Nicki would announce to the floor man that AP and I were friends with her and asked if it was okay that she deal to us. She always got the okay. She was (actually still is) an honorable person. I last spoke to her during the very last week I was allowed to play at the Bellagio, where she was dealing.

There were also the nutcases.

I remember one player who wore goggles, a leather jacket (in 110-degree heat), had feathers in his hair (they weren't pretty feathers, they looked as if they were pigeon feathers), and he played a slamming, obnoxiously loud game. When he'd take a hit, instead of scratching his cards along the felt, which is the way to ask for another card in hand-held games, he'd rub them so hard I thought the color would come off them. When he split pairs, he'd slam them down on the table. He did the same when doubling down. When he put out a bet, he'd slam the chips onto the felt. He also enjoyed clicking his chips, a habit that drove Ken Rose crazy. ("Does he have to click his damn chips? Does he have to click them? I hate clickers. Does he have to do that? I hate clickers.")

This guy annoyed me, too. He also annoyed AP, the dealers, the pit, and anyone within earshot of our table. He probably annoyed God.

Many card counters like to put on what is called "an act." They pretend to be someone who couldn't possibly be counting cards. They try to look dumb or inebriated or bored. The entire "act" is an attempt to fool the casino pit folks into believing there is no way they have an edge over the house. If goggle-eyed man was putting on an act, it was a good one. He looked insane, even though at this game no act was actually needed. The casino folks didn't care that we were counting.

Some card counters are moaners. Since they have an edge, they think they should win every session and even win every hand in positive counts in every session. I wish that were true. It would make the card-counting life so much easier than it really is (which I foolishly thought it was on that first trip to Atlantic City). The game—even the marvelous Maxim game—goes up and down, and even in highly favorable moments, you can (and will) lose hands. It's the way of the blackjack world. If you think of it as a fight, you are going to get punched even if you ultimately beat your opponent.

But the moaners don't see it that way, so they bitch along with their moaning. One guy, known as "Purple Man" because he always wore a purple shirt and a food-stained yellow tie, started moaning even before he got his first hand: "I'll bet my bad luck will continue today, too. I just can't win." Moaners are truly some of the most annoying players. Usually I ignore them—I am fairly good when it comes to blocking out the world when I play—but this one moaner finally made me speak up. I said, "You should think of giving up gambling. Looks as if you're getting an ulcer. Looks like you might die."

"With my luck," he lamented, "I'd probably linger in pain." (One can only hope.)

While the Maxim dealers were professional and friendly, there were two who didn't fit that bill. We called one dealer Muhammad Ali (because he looked like Muhammad Ali), but he had the personality of a sullen Sonny Liston. He never said thank you when we gave him a tip. He'd ignore us. He'd also ignore us if we tried to start a conversation. It was as if we were not playing at his table. It was as if we didn't exist at all. But we had to play at his table when spots were available. You don't stop playing a great game because the dealer is a jerk. In dice control, if a dealer gets on you and it rattles you, it *does* affect your game.

It got to the point where for weeks we didn't talk to him, he didn't talk to us, and we didn't tip him a penny. Sadly, the dealers pooled their tips, so the fact that Muhammad Ali was a dick probably hurt all the dealers, not just him. If you are in a profession where you have to deal with the public, then you should act as if you like them. You don't have to actually like them, but your job is to make them think you do. Muhammad Ali had no desire to act in the right way, a poor decision on his part, because he hurt every other dealer on his shift. Muhammad Ali KO'd any chance of his fellow dealers or of him making more money; he was a sullen, stupid guy.

Then there was Fred, another sullen type, although nowhere near as creepy as Muhammad Ali. Fred just wouldn't smile, even when you gave him a tip, though he would pound the tip on the metal side of the chip rack and nod his head before he put it in the chip box. I had no idea if the guy had teeth, since he didn't smile or talk to us. If we said something to him he'd nod, but that was about it. Of course, compared to Muhammad Ali, who didn't even nod, Fred was more like a charming Fred Astaire as opposed to Freddy Krueger from the *Nightmare on Elm Street* movies.

AP and I have a general rule when it comes to workers: if they give good service and are professional and friendly, we like to write letters of praise or even go to management and tell them, in front of the employee, just how great that employee is. Usually most businesses get letters of complaint or howlingly loud dissatisfied customers in person, but rarely do workers get letters of commendation or in-person praise to their superiors from their patrons.

Toward the end of our eight weeks, AP was writing down the proper spellings of the names of those dealers we played with and the floor people we liked, in order to write a letter of commendation. Fred got wind of this fact and realized we hadn't asked him for the proper spelling of his last name. That certainly changed things around.

In our eighth week at the Maxim, Fred became the happiest, most smiling dealer I had ever met. I even saw that, indeed, he did have teeth. We included him in the letter—what the hell—but for Muhammad Ali, he stayed a dickhead from beginning to end, though we did not mention that in our letter.

Midway through our eight-week stay, Paul Keen did two things: he showed me how to add to my edge and he tried to sell me a different blackjack counting system. Yes, Paul sold systems as a sideline. You do what you've got to do to make a living, I guess.

As I mentioned, the card-counting system AP and I used at the time is known as the Hi-Lo count. (This is long before there was such a thing as Speed Count, which is what I use now.) You kept track of the high cards—the 10s, jacks, queens, kings, and aces—and you kept track of the low cards—2s, 3s, 4s, 5s, and 6's. The 7s, 8s, and 9s were of neutral value, meaning no value.

You gave a point value of −1 to each of the 10-valued cards (10s, jacks, queens, and kings) and aces (which has a hand value of 1 or 11) when they came out of the deck, and you gave a point value of +1 when a small card appeared. If the deck became rich in plus-counts (meaning more small cards had been played), the player could have an edge over the house. If the count was minus, the house had an edge over the player.

That, in a nutshell, is the basic theory of card counting. (I know I am repeating myself, but I want to make sure this concept is firmly established in your mind if you are new to the idea of card counting.)

High cards remaining to be played favored the player because the player would get paid more money when he received a black-jack, which paid off at 3-to-2 even though statistically the dealer received as many blackjacks. Since the player got paid 3-to-2, an even split in blackjacks economically favored the players. In high counts, although the dealer did make his hands more often, when he showed a bust hand, he was more likely to bust with so many 10-valued cards remaining. These changes gave the player an edge, and at the Maxim game, it gave the player the highest edge I have ever seen in blackjack.

Keep in mind, the dealer plays a certain way all the time and cannot change how he takes his hits or when he must stand on a hand. His strategy is stagnant. Not so with the player. The player has no such obligation—we can change how we play certain hands based on the count at any given time.

The four of us were eating one night at the steakhouse—my treat, because AP and I had a pile of $1 coupons by this time—and this guy came over to the table and said, "Hey, hey, Paul Keen, yeah baby. That new counting system you sold me is so great. I'm winning like crazy. Thanks."

Then the guy patted Paul on the back, nodded to Susan, then to AP and me, and left the place. It did not appear as if he had eaten there; it was more like he was waiting to pounce on us when we arrived.

We ordered drinks, and when I didn't say anything about the guy, Paul jumped in and said, "Yeah, I have a better counting system than the Hi-Lo. That's what he was talking about. I sell it for $900. I can sell it to you for $400 because we've become good friends. You'll see a big difference in your winning expectation."

I couldn't believe it; this was a sales pitch!

"I'm fine with Hi-Lo," I said. "Sounds to me like your system is a multilevel system." A multilevel count system would value the cards somewhat differently. For example, a 5 might count as +2 since it is the strongest card in the deck for the dealer's ability to make a hand. All the dealer's 12s become 17, all 13s become 18, all 14s become 19, all 15s become 20, and all 16s become 21. These multilevel systems tend to be stronger than the Hi-Lo, but they take more work to master, and mistakes tend to happen more often with them.

"No, no," said Paul. "It's a single-level count."

The beautiful AP kicked me under the table as a signal that I should refrain from buying this. She knows that sometimes I am a sucker. When I went out to dinners with friends, I would always pick up the check—even if they didn't ask for it as Paul originally had. Certainly people loved to go to dinner with me because, in addition to my sparkling personality, I paid for everything. That was the Brooklyn way.

Remember that scene in *My Cousin Vinny* when Vinny is brought to his nephew's cell in prison and he tips the jail guard? Well, that was me. In Brooklyn, you picked up the checks, you gave the tips. It was a sign of manhood. It was also idiotic, as people would really take advantage of you. My philosophy from my upbringing in Brooklyn was "I tip, therefore I am." I also paid for the checks.

But not everyone shared my particular outlook. Take Silas. He was parsimonious. No, he was frugal. Actually, he was *cheap*—oh man, was he cheap! He was always happy to come to dinners with me. Seriously, while Paul Keen asked for comped meals and then paid these back by sharing his profound knowledge of the game with me, Silas gave nothing in return.

Silas' normal day went like this: He went to the buffets at breakfast and stocked up on everything he could shove in his pockets that didn't drip, melt, or spread. Whatever he took would be his lunch. If we were having dinners, especially Peter Nathan's feasts, Silas would just order white rice and then pick from others' plates: "Oh, AP, those shrimp look delicious. Can I try a couple?" "Jim, your steak looks perfectly cooked; would you cut me a slice?" "I love steamed vegetables..." "Ummm, shredded pork..." "Could I taste that dessert?" "What kind of coffee is that? Can I take a few spoonfuls to sip?"

When the check came, we would just want to split it evenly among all of us. Not so Silas. "You know," he'd say, "I only had white rice. I think it would be unfair for me to have to pay the same as everyone else."

My 50th birthday was a true testament to my eternal friendship with Silas. I was alone in Vegas during that particular trip. Silas invited me to go downtown to Michael's Steakhouse at the Four Queens, considered one of the premier steakhouses in Vegas at the time.

I knew he wouldn't pay the check for both of us, but I felt good when he asked for his own check. That was progress. I was also happy that during the meal he excused himself from the table and took the waiter aside. Now that was something. He was ordering me a cake! I felt as if I had crossed over into a parallel universe. Silas was ordering a cake as a gift for my birthday. If I had been religious, I would have thought of this as the Rapture.

After our main course, the cake arrived with candles, everyone sang "Happy Birthday," and I thanked Silas profusely after I blew out the candles. "That was really nice of you," I said. He smiled happily and nodded at my enjoyment of his surprise birthday cake with candles. When the check came, he had put the cost of it on *my* bill!

AP again kicked me under the table. That kick once again said plainly, "Do not buy Paul's system."

"Sure, Paul," I said. "I'll buy it."

I gave him the $400, and he gave me several sheets of mimeographed paper with the new counting system on it. Interesting that he had those sheets with him. It was definitely all planned ahead of time.

When we got back to the room, I immediately defended myself. "My beauty," I said. "We've made a ton of money so far. The guy needs money. What's the big deal?"

AP shook her head and replied, "You are such a soft touch."

Paul's card-counting system was not new or original. It could be found in the book *Blackjack Your Way to Riches* by Richard Albert Canfield. The system took away the 2 and ace in the count—these became neutral cards—and added the 7 as a plus card and the 9 as a minus card. In fact, my understanding is that Hi-Lo is still a better count system. There was no need for me to add those other cards to the count or make the 2 or ace neutral cards. But I paid Paul his $400. As I said to AP, "What the hell. We've learned so much from him that you can think of this as a tuition payment."

AP shook her head and then smiled. I am Cousin Vinny.

CHAPTER 5

Paul Keen Was the Greatest

During the eight weeks that AP and I played on and off with Paul Keen that summer, I gained a great appreciation for his blackjack skills. Just about anyone (who works like a feverish dog) can master the Hi-Lo card-counting system. In addition, AP and I had also mastered the end-play concept, but there was still more in the offing.

Keen took me a step further—or at least tried to take me a step further. He taught me how to follow aces and 10-valued cards through the decks.

We were at the Imperial Palace one afternoon to see the car show on the top floor of the hotel. The Imperial Palace was across the street from Caesars Palace but was not a high-end hotel or casino. In fact, when AP and I stayed there once, we considered it a dump. The car show was different; it was amazing. I am not much of a car buff, but this exhibit was truly stunning. You could see a great slice of automobile history from the chug-chug-chuggers in the earliest days to the great cars of the 1930s, '40s, '50s, and '60s.

The owner of the Imperial Palace, Ralph Engelstad, had a fascination with the Nazi era of Germany—he was often called "that Nazi nut" by many of his employees (behind his back). He had a collection of Nazi cars, including Adolph Hitler's bullet-riddled armored one. In fact, this fascination with Nazism and Hitler got Engelstad into quite a bit of trouble when employees complained that he held birthday parties for Adolph Hitler; he supposedly even invited Jewish workers to these parties. Some claimed going to the parties was mandatory, even if you were Jewish. Adding more fuel to that fire (did it really need more fuel?), Mr. Engelstad had a painting of himself in Nazi regalia looking as close to Adolph Hitler as he could make himself. Engelstad was fined $1.5 million by the Nevada Gaming Control Board for such conduct. Considering how hard it is for the Nevada Gaming Control Board to do anything against casinos and their owners, Engelstad's embarrassing love for goose-steppers obviously crossed a line.

Mr. Engelstad passed away in 2002 (some jokingly claimed he died in his bunker under the hotel). The Imperial Palace was sold to Caesars and renamed the Quad, although many people, mindful of Engelstad's reputation, now call the new place "the Clod" in his honor. Still he did have quite a great car collection. But none of my Jewish friends will ever patronize the place.

After touring the car collection, Paul said, "I want to show you a great way to add to your edge, card tracking."

The concept of card tracking (also known as shuffle tracking) is quite simple. You follow the 10-valued cards and/or the aces as they come out. When a given round is played, if there is an abundance of 10s and aces, you watch them put into the discard rack, and when the dealer finishes with all the cards, you follow the shuffle to see where those cards wind up. Then as you play, you keep your eye on those areas where the 10s and aces sit, and as they are about to be dealt on the next deal, you bet big. That is actually betting into a favorable situation. It is a step way beyond simple card counting—an extremely difficult step. Almost no card counters I ever met achieved mastery of such a technique.

Paul Keen had.

We stood behind the players at a six-deck shoe game and watched the rounds. Then it came—one round where 10s and aces poured out of the shoe. Paul watched them being played and then put into the discard rack. When the dealer finished this shoe, he took all the cards out, shuffled them, and then put the decks back into the shoe. I had no idea where those 10s and aces wound up. I tried to follow them in the shuffle, but I just couldn't do it. The shuffle became a blur to me. I couldn't believe Paul would know either. How could you follow that kind of thing? It sounded like a great method, but come on, you'd have to be Superman to do something like that. You'd need X-ray vision.

The dealer began the next round of play. Somewhere in that shoe was supposedly a clump of high cards and aces. [Maybe I shouldn't use the word *clump*, as that word has been associated with an unsavory system called, obviously enough, card clumping. Yes, debates over wording often break out in advantage-play circles.] Paul watched the discard pile. Then he nodded and said, "The next two rounds will have those 10s and aces. If we were playing, we'd pump up the bets. There should be some blackjacks and some hands of 20."

It was a miracle. Damn if a cascade of 10s and aces didn't come out in the next two rounds. Of course, there were some small cards mixed in with those 10s and aces, but there were three player blackjacks and six hands of 20 in the next two rounds.

Paul did this several times, and he always got the "clumps" of high cards correctly. Was this a perfect strategy? No. Other cards did mix in with the high cards, but overall it was a high-percentage play in favor of the player. I guessed maybe that was how Paul got that extra edge at the Maxim game because he could follow a couple or several cards even in a single-deck game. It was a thought.

Yes, Paul Keen was an elite player—truly the best I ever saw, and I have seen some other great ones. You could understand why he would be a threat to the casinos—that is, if he had enough of a bankroll with which to play. Even Paul Keen, the best blackjack player in the world, was closer to broke than break-even. He was just like Cyrano de Bergerac, the swashbuckling poet, player, and swordsman who was also almost destitute.

Cyrano was skilled in many areas, but he was a man with one serious physical flaw—a gigantic nose—and one serious psychological leaning: great pride, bordering on hubris; he could not even bow down before the aristocracy of his time. If you ever get a chance to see the play *Cyrano de Bergerac* by Edmond Rostand, run to see it. It is one of the best plays ever written.

Interestingly enough, *Cyrano de Bergerac* was Paul Keen's favorite play. The two of us would exchange quotes from the play when we were together. I had a simple reason for knowing the play by heart: I taught it to my high school honors classes. Keen knew the play because I think he believed that in the world of blackjack and Las Vegas, he was Cyrano. (I don't know the play by heart anymore, so should we ever meet, don't bandy dialogue with me. My "panache" has deserted me.)

Keen's poverty just didn't allow him to play up to his potential. With the casinos banning him or at the very least banning his high bets, his spectacular early career ended with a whimper. Paul's lack of legitimate work experience meant he did not have enough money to play at a decent income-producing level. So there was blackjack's greatest player, our Cyrano de Bergerac, on the lowest rung of the economic ladder. Such is the sad irony of life. No books would be written about his great adventures. No young players would think, *I want to be the next Paul Keen*. No great gambling writers would flock to Vegas to pick his brain. He was Ozymandias, a broken, wind-whipped statue in the desert.

Paul Keen died in the late 1990s. He either slipped in the shower, hit his head, and passed away or had a heart attack, a stroke, or a fainting spell and then hit his head. I really don't know exactly, because after our summer together, I more or less lost track of Paul Keen, though I did see him occasionally at the Gamblers Book Shop. But after a while he was never there when I was there.

CHAPTER 6

Those Devastating Scobletes

The Maxim Summer, as we came to call it, not only allowed us to meet the greatest blackjack player, but it also put the beautiful AP and me into a different category. We went from being red-chip players ($5) to green-chip players ($25) to black-chip players ($100) and sometimes even purple-chip players ($500), all in an eight-week period. Keep in mind, those large-denomination chips were in high counts that favored us.

Our playing days at the Maxim were routine. We'd get down to the casino around 6:00 AM when the tables were mostly empty. The night crowd tended to leave somewhere just before 5:00 AM. We'd play two or three hours, eat breakfast, and then play another couple hours. Then we'd head across the street to Bally's and use their exercise facilities for about an hour and a half. Then back to the hotel for a light lunch, then to our room for a nap (or, often, an *ahum* and then a nap).

After the nap, we'd head down to the casino. It would be somewhere around 3:00–4:00 PM by then, and we'd put in another couple hours. Then dinner.

Some nights we would play after dinner, but usually the casino started to get too crowded and we couldn't get spots at the single-deck tables, so we would go downtown to play low-limit craps. Although I was attempting to control the dice that summer, my success rate was dismal. I stayed as a $5 dice controller and kept practicing when I was not playing blackjack. Dice control had not yet become a "marketable" skill in my playing life—though I had been playing with two of the greatest dice controllers in the world in Atlantic City: the Captain and the Arm. I needed a lot of time to master that skill.

Our last night of the Maxim Summer saw us hammering the casino, one of our best nights of our eight-week stay. I've mentioned that some nights you win, some you lose, some you win big, and some you lose big—and some you go into a heavenly never-never land because everything you do turns out right.

That was our last night at the Maxim—our last night at the Maxim ever, in fact. On our next trip, during that Christmas, the Maxim single-deck game was long gone and the casino had slid back into the garbage heap of blackjack history.

As we colored up that last night, the pit boss, John, sidled over. We had gotten friendly with him—unlike some of my dealings with casino suits during my years of play—and we'd had great conversations. (Yes, you can talk and count cards at the same time.) I told him it would be our last night.

"How can you leave this game?" he asked.

"We did okay," I said, trying to pretend we hadn't slaughtered them.

He laughed. "I know what you've done, Frank, and that's why I'm asking, how can you leave *this* game?"

"I've got to get back to New York; my other career is calling me," I said.

"You should retire from that," he laughed. "You keep going as you're going and you won't need to teach."

"Maybe I could buy a casino," I said. "I'd make you the casino manager."

"Remember that when you buy your casino," he laughed.

How much money did we win? Here's how much: when we got back to our room, we took out all the wads of hundreds we had, opened the rubber bands, dumped the money on the bed, and the beautiful AP and I jumped and rolled and thrashed on the bed, in all that money. You've probably seen this scene in movies, but we did it in real life—before I ever saw it in a movie. It was probably unhygienic rolling around in all that dough, but it was a hell of a lot of fun.

Of course, being the overly cautious type, I was worried about carrying all that money through the Las Vegas airport, then onto the plane, through Kennedy Airport in New York, and then home. I certainly didn't want to put it into a suitcase. Someone could just lift that and run off. (How they would know it was filled with money, I have no idea. I think I thought at the time that everyone had X-ray vision like Superman.)

So the beautiful AP sewed the money into my suit. I was thin in those days, but my suit, wadded with money, made me look like the Incredible Hulk. We got the money home with no problems. In that eight-week trip, we made our first killing as a blackjack team. The only other time I made such a score was a single night when my mentor, the late Captain, had a 147-number roll in Atlantic City, but that would come 14 years later.

* * *

The beautiful AP and I became a great card-counting team throughout the 1990s, thanks to the early thrust of that Maxim Summer. We often spent close to 130 days a year in the casinos of Atlantic City and Las Vegas. When Tunica became a gambling venue, we'd head to Mississippi as well.

John, the pit person from Maxim, was wrong about that Maxim Summer allowing me to retire from teaching. Even when my gambling books became best sellers, my outlay was a little more than just my teaching or book-writing career could handle. Between AP's and my teaching salaries, my article and book sales, *and* our casino play, we were finally able to buy a house, buy a car, and send both of my sons to a private high school and then college. Everything the beautiful AP said to me on the beach in Cape May on that summer day was coming true. I was on my way up.

We started to call our summer trips to Las Vegas "the tuition runs," and that is literally what they were. We needed to make money to bring home. They were not summer vacations; they were summer jobs. Winter vacations such as Christmas and winter break became winter jobs. Easter was our spring job.

You might think spending every summer in Vegas and almost every weekend and school vacation in Atlantic City would be loads of fun. Not so. Yes, there were fine dinners, good workouts, good shows, and interesting friendships, but the pressure to win was overwhelming—we couldn't afford to lose. Not being able to afford to lose shines a totally different light on a Las Vegas experience.

I am sure many of you have seen those wildly outrageous Vegas comedies where drunken, unshaven louts let it all hang out in the city of sin and indulgence. That is one of the two images Vegas (and all casinos) like to foster—wild abandonment of civilization in a frenzied whirl fueled by booze, sex, and idiocy. The second image is the reverse, with genteel, happy, good-looking people with scads of money enjoying a delightful pastime in an elegant way, sipping their martinis. At least those were the images you'd see in the advertisements. You never saw a blue-haired old lady aimlessly playing slots as if she were a zombie, or some drunken man with cigarette ashes on his shirt and drool slowly making its way down his chin.

Those two distinct casino images were the exact opposite of our Vegas and Atlantic City careers. We were closer to being the Amish version of Las Vegas than the let-it-all-hang-out version. While we did treat ourselves to fine restaurants and the occasional show, we had to work hard because playing blackjack was hard work. I think most card counters will confirm that.

Vegas has never been—even now that our kids are in their mid-30s and I am not under the gun to win anymore—a vacation spot for us. The city is a Christmas ornament, surely, but it is not a real tree. It is a façade, and that is all I see of the city—the make-believe. I am just too experienced and too cynical to fall for the glitz and supposed glamour of it all. Playing blackjack *from need* changed the whole nature of Sin City for me, and even more so for AP. In fact, if she never sets foot on Nevada soil again, it would not bother her one bit. "I'll wave when I fly over on my way to Hawaii," she says.

But in "those days" we had no choice. Need constantly propelled us. Vegas had the best games, and when Christmas, winter break, and Easter came around, we were on planes flying to our part-time jobs. The summer was always the major "tuition run."

And without bragging (much), I must say we were highly successful. AP and I created a great way to play. At root, after the Maxim Summer, I generally played two hands and made the bets; AP did the counting and signaled me what the count was.

We had an elaborate system of signals—both verbal and physical—that she would use to alert me to the count. For example, if AP talked about the president and his wife doing something (or any couple or pair doing or saying something or two movies she wanted to see), the count was a +2, since a couple equaled two; if she told me I was drinking too much or I needed some water so I wouldn't become dehydrated, asked for a sip of water, or talked about how much you sweated in such hot weather, the count was a +7, as in 7&7 the drink. If she touched my forearm, the count was a +4, or if she mentioned any boxer, it was also a +4 (in honor of George Foreman). There were a few hundred possible signals, and they could be slipped into any conversation or be understood depending on what part of my or her body was touched. The conversations could be with me, with the dealer, the waitress, the floor person, or the pit boss.

Since the low counts were not as essential because the bet would usually be minimal, we tended only to have signals in minus counts that indicated the counts were three points lower than neutral. For instance, "The casino is crowded tonight" or, "The casino isn't as crowded tonight." Number of people meant we were in the minus counts. Crowded meant we were lower than –3; not so crowded was at –1 or –2, give or take a fraction. I liked to know a general idea of the minus counts in order to change my playing strategy. But this was not an important count or aspect of our play. The key to winning money at blackjack is getting the big bets out there when you have the decided advantage; all other things are secondary.

We had layer upon layer of signals. Those I listed are just a few. The beautiful AP would count, signal me, and I played the hands and did the betting. As all this was going on, I was talking to the dealer, the floor person, the pit boss. I barely looked at the cards. I drank. I had "fun." I'm paying for that fun now. I gained 100 pounds during my casino playing career, from the early 1990s to April 2012. If I were still in acting, I would have gone from the sexy, svelte leading man who enjoyed taking his shirt off to show his body all the way to the fat and funny neighbor with man problems.

Anyway, that was our usual method of playing, though we sometimes changed things depending on the game we were playing. I never did master shuffle tracking, but we tended to stick to single-deck and double-deck games. I tried to practice the shuffle tracking; I just couldn't do it. I did, however, discover some new blackjack strategies that I never wrote about until recently. One was the "fat finger" strategy.

For several years some Las Vegas casinos—mostly the Mirage properties—offered a two-deck game dealt faceup. This was unusual, as most double-deckers are dealt facedown. You will probably find some casinos throughout the country that continue to do the faceup double-deck game, and if so, the "fat finger" strategy can give you a startlingly large advantage.

The ultimate spot on the table is at first base for the "fat finger" strategy, so when you see that a dealer is falling into "fatitude," you must get yourself to first base. (First base is the very first seat to the dealer's left and is the first position to get cards.)

So here is how this technique works: the dealer deals the cards to the players faceup. When the dealer gets to third base (immediately to the dealer's right) and he starts to flip the card over for the player, there are times when he double flips—that is, he starts to flip two cards at the same time. In a normal deal, the top card is the player's, but in a double flip, the dealer shows the second card accidentally; that card will be the dealer's hole card. The dealer catches the almost-mistake and, knowing he was about to show his hole card, quickly stops the flip and fixes the cards so the player gets the correct card without the dealer's hole card being seen or being flipped. *Or so he thinks.*

That hole card is often visible from first base. That's right; he isn't able to hide the card completely from the first-base player, meaning you. Now you know his hole card and can play your hands with that knowledge. You have just had a huge edge given to you on a golden plate.

What makes this a great way to play has to do with some of the hitting and standing decisions that you can make. If you know the dealer has a 6 under his up-card of 10, you might want to stand on your 15s and 16s or double on your 9s. He will not know that you know he has a 6 in the hole. Your playing decisions can really help you bring in the money. Of course, you could go completely nuts with your decisions. You would be foolish to stand on a 12 against a dealer's 10 card even if you knew the dealer had a 6 in the hole. That would be something of a giveaway. You have to keep yourself somewhat reined in so the pit isn't aware of the fact that you are not actually dumb (as you appear to be, based on your strategies) but actually smart enough to catch a problem in their game. Smart is bad in a casino; dumb is prized.

Obviously, the reason I call this the "fat finger" strategy has to do with which dealers tend to make this misstep. Sure, at times all types of dealers make this mistake, but the large, thick-fingered ones make it the most. Be thankful so many Americans are out of shape and overweight or nicely plump due to so much sugar and fat in our diets!

The best dealer I ever had was at Bellagio; he double-flipped almost 10 percent of the time. Still, I didn't go all out to take hits.

If I had an 18 or 19, I stayed on my hand even though I knew the dealer had, say, a 20. Again, hitting an 18 or 19 would be too radical a hit unless you look like Alfred E. Neuman and have drool dripping down your chin.

I did, however, double-down on hands such as a 9 against a dealer's 10 up-card when I knew he had a small card in the hole. This merely looked as if I were stupid, whereas hitting on an 18 or 19 would have made me look crazy or smart. Again, casinos love stupid. Also, crazy gives the casino pit people pause.

AP and I played these faceup two-deck games for more than a year, and it was a very, very satisfying year indeed. Money was made, tuitions got paid. And AP and I paid off our mortgage in seven years, to boot!

At the original Aladdin casino, before the hotel was torn down and made into the new Aladdin casino, which was then sold and made into Planet Hollywood, I used a "shiny coin" technique to catch a glimpse of the dealer's hole card. Instead of having $1 white (or blue) chips, the Aladdin used slot coins. Some of these were not the grimy, fingered ones that went in and out of the machines, but coins that (I assume) were basically only used for blackjack. (Coins were not real coins, but slot coins.)

As the dealer would slide his hole card under his up-card, occasionally you could get a quick peek at it. The picture cards were easy to spot even if you couldn't always tell which ones they were—the massive coloration and the lines at the top told you that the dealer had a 10-valued card in the hole. It was not as easy to distinguish the other cards as readily.

As AP and I made our sweep of the old Aladdin before we played, I always looked to see if those slot coins were shiny enough to give me a glimpse of the hole card. Sometimes they were, sometimes they weren't. It never hurt to look.

Obviously during our casino runs we used match play, aces play (the casino gives you a free ace to be used whenever you want), and whatever other "play" the casinos generously awarded. We took everything we could take and gave them as little as we could give.

Our goal was simple. We wanted to take the casinos the same way the casinos took all those players who just threw their money away on "fun and good times," as one of my acquaintances once said. I don't know how you can have "fun and good times" after coming home having lost about $7,000. Fun and good times? For us? Nope. Just show us the money! That was fun. That was a good time.

CHAPTER 7

The Long Run

Many of you have heard the expression "the long run" when it comes to casino games. The long run is the number of decisions where the real and probabilistic percentages start to converge. Take a coin flip. You do 10 of these, and although the math says it is a 50/50 situation, often the real-world results will be heavily skewed toward one or the other. You could have seven heads and three tails or nine tails and one head. But as you do more and more trials, going into the millions, you will find that the real world begins to look more and more like the mathematical or probabilistic model. You might find the coin flip favoring heads at 50.09 percent–to–49.91 percent. Even during millions of flips, it would be improbable that the split would be 50/50, but the percentages would come somewhat close to that. Blackjack math tends to deal with the long-run percentages. But how long is the long run, and can anyone meet the long run in his playing career? The answer is, I haven't got the faintest idea. I think the actual long run in blackjack is heavily influenced by elements that can't be put into mathematical formulas, such as discovering someone who had the "fat finger" tendency or following 10s and aces through a shuffle. It is hard to mathematize such things. (Have I just invented a word: mathematize?)

Even if we discount all the eccentric ways to get an edge, you only have one real way to play your game outside of such eccentricity: the way the math tells you to play. There is no such thing as a valid short-run strategy—unless you catch the dealer's hole card or can follow 10s and aces through a shuffle, etc. The long run for those skills is pretty short—like the next round of cards being dealt. But the long run for card counting is—well—pretty long.

If you look at the Maxim Summer and postulate that AP and I played four hands per round (two hands each) with 100 decisions for each hand per hour and eight hours per day, we played roughly 180,000 to 200,000 hands that summer (about 2 percent of the hands were probably splits). Add in another 10 years of play—not just summers, but vacations and weekends—and you can see we were probably well over 2 million hands. Was that the long run? I'm guessing the playing reality was close to the mathematical probabilities, that with that many hands, good card counters are (almost) guaranteed a winning record.

Of course, even after the beautiful AP retired, I played another 10 years before I went into semi-retirement from blackjack, keeping my playing time now limited almost exclusively to craps (using dice control) and Pai Gow poker (using the techniques that can be found in my book *Everything Casino Poker: Get the Edge at Video Poker, Texas Hold'em, Omaha Hi-Lo, and Pai Gow Poker!*)

I've played a lot of blackjack hands in a lot of casinos over a lot of years. I've played games where the dealers have exposed their hole cards; where dealers have made mistakes in my favor; where promotions have given me free aces, match plays, even free chips. I've played blackjack games that mistakenly gave players the edge because the casino executives who brought the games in didn't realize the games were faulty. I've gotten tremendous comps at casinos where I was able to hide my counting from the casino bosses.

In short, the beautiful AP and I did it together—we beat the casinos at blackjack. I was also able to do it alone. It created my favorite saying, which I coined in the early 1990s: *Winning is the most fun!*

But some card counters are overwhelmed with the desire to get into the long run as quickly as possible. That included a couple we met at the Frontier casino in the mid-1990s. This husband-and-wife team—he was Italian; she was Korean—had read Stanford Wong's excellent book *Professional Blackjack* and started their pursuit of a blackjack fortune. But first, "We must get into the long run," they both would say.

Since they lived in California, they were able to go to Vegas every weekend and they played nonstop until (I guess) they collapsed from exhaustion. We called them "the Long Run Couple."

During the summer we met them, the Frontier had a great single-deck blackjack game that AP and I played frequently during different shifts. We played different shifts so the suits wouldn't see us so much that they would get suspicious. The only problem we had with the Frontier was a monstrous labor dispute they were having with the Culinary Union. That dispute lasted from 1991 to 1998, and at times it became rather heated (to say the least) as picketers protested outside the casino 24 hours a day.

To get into the casino, you had to cross a picket line of people who were often so angry they would growl at you. Once AP tried to explain to one woman, "You don't understand, we can beat their blackjack games, so that's why we play." That woman snarled and sneered. Two days later that same woman had an open battle with another person right in the middle of Las Vegas Blvd. As a former union head, I could understand the plight of the workers, but as a blackjack player, I was only interested in one thing: taking the Frontier's money. Had I been a regular gambler, ultimately giving my money to the casinos by playing unbeatable games, I would never have crossed the picket line. I could lose my money in a casino where there was no union-management strife.

But strike or no strike, growling picketers or no growling picketers, the two of us went where the best games were being dealt. We played the Frontier for several years until their blackjack game deteriorated.

The Long Run Couple would be at the Frontier in the morning when we arrived—around 6:00. They would be there in the afternoon, too and they would be there at night. Unlike the beautiful AP and me, they weren't just playing separate shifts, they were playing all the shifts all day and most of the night, too. By Sunday, they looked like dirty dishrags. Getting into the long run seemed to be killing them. How they ever drove back to California in the wee hours of Monday morning was beyond me. I wondered how they were ever able to work. I just hoped he or she weren't brain surgeons or bus drivers. I often felt like taking a nap for them.

There is no doubt that when you have the edge, the more decisions you play the better the chance that you'll be ahead. But aside from the health consequences that the Long Run Couple might have experienced, playing for seemingly endless hours will generate another problem: when you are fatigued, you make mistakes and you often don't realize that you are making those mistakes. Mistakes can kill your edge. Mistakes can often take that edge almost down to nothing. Mistakes can sometimes give the edge right back to the casino.

The edge in blackjack, even for the best counters, is relatively small, maybe between ½ to 2 percent, and to realize that edge, you have to play super smart and super aware. Fatigue can hammer such smartness and awareness. I think the Long Run Couple would have been far better off just getting a full night's sleep. Living in California, they had ample opportunity to get in millions of hands over the years, so why not make those hands where no mistakes would be made?

That concept of being well rested was hammered home to me by the Captain when I talked to him after our disastrous second trip to Atlantic City. "You don't think clearly when you're tired," he said. "You'll take chances you wouldn't take if you were well rested. Those chances can cripple you."

He was right. In those days, Atlantic City was not 24/7 as it is now; they closed for several hours during the early morning and opened somewhere around 10:00 AM. And I would be standing there when those gates opened to try to win back my money. I was betting like a wild man, too. If the count even favored me a little, my larger bets became way too large. Did I make other mistakes because of fatigue? I made so many mistakes that their name was legion. I needed a blackjack exorcist, so much had the devil of fatigue possessed me.

Where is the Long Run Couple today? I wonder if trying to reach the long run did them in. Are they sitting somewhere in a rest home, giggling, their eyes spinning while they slobber to the nurses, "We made it to the long run; we made it to the long run."

CHAPTER 8

Assorted Nuts

We spent quite a bit of time with Ken Rose, Peter Nathan, Silas, and someone I called "Wheat Germ Man" (more about him later in this chapter) when they were in town during the early 1990s. Nathan played blackjack well, and he was not afraid to put out the big bets when the count called for them. The big bets were the bets that won you the money in the long run because they were the bets when you had the edge.

On the other hand, both Ken Rose and especially Silas had real trouble putting those big bets out. Rose continued to play at the $5 level, even though he could afford far higher stakes—he should have been a $100 or a $500 player. No problem there, of course; his betting level was his choice. His problem was that he couldn't push himself to go with a one-bet-to-four-bet spread in the single-deck games or one-to-six in two-deck games. He just couldn't bet $20 or $30 at one shot.

Okay, that was bad. It reduced his ability to really nail the house over time. He just couldn't be brought to make larger bets; there was no "get the money out there" for him. I mentioned in the foreword that some advantage players just can't think of chips as just chips; they see the money value behind them.

It is an interesting contrast between advantage players and typical gamblers when it comes to valuing casino chips. In books and articles that I gear toward non-advantage players I pound out

61

the point that you must think of your chips and your credits on a slot machine as actual money, money you have earned. You should never just think of them as chips or credits. But with advantage players, the whole thing is reversed. You must not worry about the fact that a purple chip is $500—if the count calls for you to bet that purple chip, you bet it. Why? Because it is *only* a purple chip. Naturally you need a large total bankroll to bet such purple chips, but you get the point. In favorable counts, the card counter has to bet those chips and not think of them as money. And what about me? I had no trouble betting the chips; but sadly, I always did think of them as money. I wish I could take my own advice!

Silas was far, far worse. He found it hard to increase his bets at all. Silas was one of the best counters I knew, but his stinginess and big mouth (with shiny wet lips) made playing beside him a chore. He'd *loudly* mention that you were pushing your bet up. "Hey, hey, Frank, you going for the gold with that big bet?" I have no idea why he was so stupid as to do that. Maybe he was punishing me for something he didn't have the balls to do.

This loud broadcast brought undue attention from the pit. A couple of times it got me barred, which is a polite form of banning, meaning you can come to the casino to play slots or other table games but no more blackjack would be allowed. I would tell Silas to shut up when we were at the tables, but invariably he'd keep doing it. Finally I had to tell him that if he kept it up, AP and I were done with him. He stopped. Instead, he decided he'd get a woman and become a team just like the beautiful AP and me.

"You guys know what you're doing," he said. "I get myself a woman partner, and we take on those casinos, baby."

It was evident to my friends and acquaintances that AP and I had something good going—that "something" certainly encompassed playing as a team in blackjack but it also encompassed a deep and abiding love between us. We had fun together. Indeed, to this very moment, we still have fun together. She's the best date in the world.

Silas put an ad in a California newspaper saying he wanted a female blackjack playing partner, "no experience necessary." He'd teach the woman how to play and how to count. She just had to be receptive to studying hard because there would be many trips to Las Vegas.

He got several women to apply—oh, yes, he had a written application—and after he interviewed them thoroughly, he picked the one he wanted: the prettiest one. He spent a week or so teaching her basic strategy and another few weeks teaching her how to count cards. During this time, they "dated"—I put "dated" in quotes because Silas' idea of a date would probably not be your idea. Silas liked to go to dinner and a show. Dinner was dutch with him buying his white rice and the woman ordering a normal dinner, of which Silas would eat half. Then off to the show...maybe.

Silas didn't have tickets. He'd go outside theaters where the scalpers needed to dump their unsold seats—therefore these tickets were dirt cheap. Often the shows had received mediocre or bad reviews, sticking the scalpers with tickets because few people wanted to see those shows. So even with the best seats in the house bought for an incredibly low amount, many of the shows just weren't all that good. If he couldn't score tickets, they would go back to her apartment and watch television. I think it goes without saying—but I'll say it anyway—his blackjack partner always had to pay for her own tickets.

Finally they showed up in Vegas to join AP and me. The lady, who *begged* me not to use her name ("I don't want my name associated with that bastard"), was a smart, cute, accomplished elementary school teacher. I think she was looking for a meaningful relationship that might lead to marriage. She was probably also looking for enjoyable times in Las Vegas—at least Las Vegas sounds as if it should be enjoyable.

Instead here is what she got: In the morning Silas took her to the Rio Buffet, which during the 1990s was inexpensive and delicious. (It is still delicious.) Silas would stuff his pockets and her purse with food—this food was to be for the rest of the day and evening, unless they went out to dinner with AP and me, where he could order his white rice and eat *our* food. The lady was not happy going out to eat once a day or stuffing her purse with food from a buffet that cost $3.95. She was not happy that Silas did not want to go to any shows or discos. She was also not happy that Silas only wanted to eat out in the morning. She was not happy that Silas busted her chops if she made the least mistake while playing in the casinos. (He'd take her outside and reprimand her: "You were a point off in that count. You have to pay attention. Money is at stake.") She was not happy at the lower-level hotels Silas preferred staying in. She once whispered sarcastically, "Some of these hotels aren't as nice as the dumpsters behind them."

She did help Silas in one way. While she was his short-lived partner, Silas was able to up his bet one-to-four in single-deck games and one-to-six in double-deck games. That was a true breakthrough for him. But this card-counting team didn't last long.

In a fit of anger in the middle of Las Vegas Blvd., between the old Desert Inn and the old Frontier, this sweet, young elementary school teacher told Silas to "go to hell" when he informed her casually that she owed him $22 for something or other. She flew back to California that day and sent Silas a check for $22 made out to "Silas, the cheapest man in the world!"

Silas couldn't get over it. "I just don't get it," he said. "Women are really something, aren't they? I taught her how to play blackjack, and this is how she treats me. Women are crazy." Needless to say, when last I heard, Silas had not married.

Once Silas shut up at the tables, I really didn't care if he ate one meal a day or stuffed his pockets with buffet food or slept in a dumpster or put his wet lips on some prostitute at the Mustang Ranch. AP and I just stopped asking him to go out with us, and that limited our social time with him—and it also allowed us to actually eat the entire meals we ordered. I couldn't stop him from hooking up with me at the casinos because he knew the dozen or so casinos where I played.

Invariably AP and I would be playing, and then Silas would plop himself down at the table, cash in, and not play correctly. Why someone who had the bucks, enjoyed playing blackjack, and could count cards perfectly would not do what you had to do to get the real edge was beyond me.

There are some people who cause other people not to want to be with them—that was Silas—and these people also cause other people not to want to be with the friends of those people—that was also Silas. I was discovering that the more I had Silas with me, the less I saw my other friends. Silas was like garlic to vampires. As a friend, he also was no great shakes. In fact, I never considered him a friend, merely an annoying acquaintance.

If Silas was annoying, the Wheat Germ Man was totally whacked out. First, he was a great card counter—not as good as Paul Keen, but in that elite category nevertheless. He had some three-level count, and he could also track cards in the decks but not with the precision of Keen. He was fearless in getting his big bets out when the count favored him. He was an all-around pro. He would be what any blackjack player wishes to be—talented, perceptive to dealer mistakes, fearless.

And he was thoroughly insane.

I called him "the Wheat Germ Man" because he was a health-food fanatic—his favorite drink was some concoction of wheat grass and Gatorade. He was completely convinced that such a drink prevented cancers—all kinds of cancers, too—along with heart attacks, strokes, and body sores and thought such a concoction would prolong his life into his early 100s. "I will be the healthiest 100-year-old in the world. That is my intention," he would say.

His breakfast was wheat germ with banana and a whole grove of other fruit. Or oatmeal with the same grove of fruit. He took far more vitamins than I did—and I am basically a vitamin junkie. I would say he took a handful every couple hours. He also loved seaweed, even that stinking raw seaweed just out of the ocean. He gave himself enemas just about every day.

"Enemas are great for cleansing you," he'd say. "I use decaffeinated coffee, as I find that cleans me out without the jangling from the caffeine."

He ate almost no meat and he loved fish.

I met him in 1995 during the Christmas vacation. During Christmas many of the big billboards at Caesars, Las Vegas Hilton, and other major properties were written in Chinese. Vegas was crowded with Asians during Christmas. Wheat Germ Man was not a fan of Asian players.

He would say things like, "These Orientals—and I call them Orientals, doesn't that sound exotic instead of Asians? I think so. What's with this Asian crap? They don't know how to play. They're morons, but they come to the table and throw their money around and yell in that stupid language. Why don't they just shut up and play the slots? They don't know how to play, so why waste everyone's time? I can't stand them coming to the table and jabbering like monkeys. If they don't know how to play, they should go away."

Wheat Germ Man was rarely in a good mood. Everyone was a moron or—if they were of another race—a monkey to him. He always had something to complain about. He always had something to lecture you about. He believed he knew everything.

He thought he knew more about health and medicine than doctors. He thought he knew more about government than any political science professor in America. His opinion of college political science professors: "They are all lackeys of the power structure. When the revolution comes, they will all be broken eggs in the university system. In the revolution to make an omelet, you have to break some eggs. I'll have my baseball bat." He was also convinced that there were giant worldwide conspiracies. Some of these were among countries, some among politicians, rich people, Catholics, Jews, illuminati, masons, and maybe even bricklayers.

He was a high school dropout. He once said, "School is stupid. Look at how many stupid people have gone to school and graduated. More stupid people have graduated than smart people."

And he almost always had a cold or, as he said, "allergies" to the poisons around us. He was sniffling, coughing, incessantly blowing gobs of greenish mucus into tissues that tended to rip apart when such heavy loads were propelled into them. It was kind of like watching a movie called *The Blob from the Outer Nostrils*.

The daily enemas gave him a raging case of ulcerative colitis—a disease that is horribly painful and debilitating. The ulcerative colitis came about—according to the emergency room doctor who treated this anally bleeding, dehydrated, hallucinating shell of a health-food expert—from those enemas over so many years. The doctor explained that Wheat Germ Man probably had a genetic predisposition to the disease, but his enemas and stress probably brought that factor out, and that is what landed him in the emergency room.

When a strong regimen of prednisone, a steroid, halted the symptoms, thereby easing his pain, Wheat Germ Man returned to the blackjack wars and he told us, "What the hell do those doctors know? They wouldn't give me the [wheat grass] juice and Gatorade. They pumped me full of drugs. They're all morons in a conspiracy with the FDA. My body, being healthy, cured itself." Then he blew his green globule into his tissue. The fact that modern medicine might have saved his life was irrelevant. Wheat Germ Man's famous saying was, "Who you gonna believe? Me or the FDA?"

I sometimes wonder why so many of the great blackjack players I've met seem to have personality disorders—at least what seem to me to be personality disorders. Certainly, Wheat Germ Man fit right into that diagnosis. He was a health nut who was unhealthy, a high school dropout who knew everything, and an anti-"Oriental"...still, he was a marvelous blackjack player.

His saying was a simple, "Get the money out there," which I've since appropriated. I use it all the time. And he did get the money out there. If you want to be a successful card counter, Wheat Germ Man—for all his madness—hit the nail on the head: get the money out there.

He died in 2001 at the age of 38.

* * *

I also met up with some Hollywood folks—not big Hollywood folks, just little folks who wanted to be big folks. They all seemed to have totally exaggerated views of themselves. One guy was always quoting from his screenplays: "As I said in my screenplay *The Total Animal*, human beings are total animals. No one can disagree with that, but the studios don't think this would be a good subject for a lightweight family comedy. There's only a little nudity." This guy was serious, too.

Another Hollywoodie thought he should be given a job as a director. He often said, "I can do a better job than those yahoos directing now." When asked how many films he had directed, he said, "None yet, but I'm waiting for the call." When asked how many films he'd been involved with, he said, "Do you think that I would lower myself to do most films? I'm waiting for the call." When asked who would call, he said, "Any of the big companies, and then I would negotiate a deal. But I will not do any television. That's beneath me."

He was a $5 player with delusions of grandeur. He was also on some form of Social Security disability and was receiving other aid from the state of California. I think the only call he would be getting in the future would be from the Department of Mental Health.

Yes, I am having some fun with some of these memories. Not everyone I met was a lunatic; most of the card counters were really just average Janes and Joes who enjoyed playing the game with an edge. Still, it would be interesting to do a survey of what percentage of the blackjack card-counting population had mental illness or at the very least an overblown opinion of themselves as compared to a random sampling of the general population. Of course, I really have no idea of how to do such a survey. And I am probably wrong about my thesis; maybe there are a lot more nuts in the general population than I think.

As the 1990s progressed, I made the acquaintance of many famous gambling writers, players, and researchers. I read just about every blackjack book that was published. I enjoyed and learned from many books, be they new methods of advantage play, new mathematical analyses, or works that were personal in nature and gave the history and play of individuals.

I am not a computer buff. I am not a mathematician. When I need to find out how this or that aspect of blackjack or any gambling game works, I call on experts such as Don Catlin, Jerry "Stickman," John "Skinny," Dan Pronovost, Henry Tamburin, and others. I am a writer and a player, but I am well aware of my weaknesses, and I handle those weaknesses by seeking the help of those who know more than I do about math and computer programming.

To be a good card counter or a good dice controller, you do not have to be a mathematical genius or a Rain Man. You do not have to know how the clock is built; you just have to know how to tell the time. Just about anyone who really wants it can get an edge over the casinos. It does take work, but it also took work to get the money you wish to gamble with.

CHAPTER 9

Playing with Blackjack Teams

Certainly the casinos can still be beaten in blackjack by individuals playing alone, but you have to really know what you are doing and do something different than what the casinos expect. The old counting systems, such as Hi-Lo, are not as easy to get away with as they used to be, and the games being offered are nowhere near as good as the games I played in the 1990s. Most of today's single-deck games only pay 6-to-5 on a blackjack—whereas the traditional games paid 3-to-2. Most games now have the dealer hit soft 17; some restrict doubling and splitting. The casinos are looking to squeeze every last penny from non-advantage players. Their new rules are not good for card counters either. And casino paranoia reigns supreme in many places. Blackjack is beatable, but it does take astute dedication and a rejection of playing any old game because that game is the only one you can find.

The new counting system, Speed Count (see my book *Beat Blackjack Now!: The Easiest Way to Get the Edge!*), is unique in many of its aspects, and I would recommend it to anyone just starting out in the blackjack card-counting arena. It plays a lot differently than the traditional counts, although it is not quite as strong. This is a count system that you can probably get away with easier than with other traditional counts.

(In the appendixes you will find the Hi-Lo model of card counting, the Paul Keen card-counting system, and an overview of Speed Count.) Obviously, to get good at any one of these requires work.

One aspect of blackjack play that has become extremely popular in the modern media is the idea of playing with teams of players, either pooling the bankroll and dividing that into shares, or paying others to play for you by giving them an hourly wage.

Many readers and movie patrons have become familiar with the great MIT blackjack teams of the 1990s and early 2000s composed of college and graduate students who descended on Vegas and supposedly won millions of dollars. Their stories chronicle fun adventures of intrigue and high living, the stuff of which Vegas dreams are made—those Ken Uston type of dreams. In reality these "college teams" go all the way back to the late 1970s. Team play might be just as old as any other type of advantage blackjack play.

Certainly playing on blackjack teams is an entirely different type of animal than playing singly or with just one partner, as I did with my wife. Team play has all the problems of any team activity jointly engaged in by people with a strong agenda. That agenda being the making of money in blackjack play. Check out sporting teams, research teams, or Little League teams and you'll find one certain thing: where there are people, there can be problems. I've been involved in team play as well—separate and apart from my play with the beautiful AP—and while I have found them to be (generally) good investments, the "people problems" sometimes overwhelm the money-making potential. Yes, hell certainly can be "other people."

There are generally two types of teams: those that call in a "big player" when the count gets positive and those that spread out and play individually at different tables and/or casinos. I guess you could say there is a third type that is merely a combination of the first two types.

The "big player" model had its first public exposure in 1977 when the book *The Big Player: How a Team of Blackjack Players*

Made a Million Dollars by Ken Uston and Roger Rapoport was published. This book recounted the amazing adventures of blackjack's
most famous and flamboyant player, the late, great Ken Uston. It
is a book that is still exciting and fun to read, and I recommend it
highly. Although a word of caution here: don't try to imitate Ken
Uston. He was the one and *only* Ken Uston.

A team of players spreads out in a casino at different tables
and counts down the decks. When the count gets positive—positive
enough that the good cards should last a round or two or more—a
signal is given to the "big player," who is lounging around, usually
at the bar, and this player comes rushing over to the table to put
down a substantial wager. By betting in this way, the casino is not
aware that this big player is actually a card counter and a member
of a card-counting team. He merely appears to be a typical (perhaps
tipsy) high roller playing his hunches and betting up a storm.

Ken Uston was that big player. Some think he was the ultimate
big player—much as folks think of Babe Ruth as the ultimate
baseball player.

Born Kenneth Senzo Usui in 1935, Uston went to college at
the tender age of 16—Yale University, no less. He then received
an MBA from Harvard University. He was a gifted musician as well
and often played jazz clubs in California. So add him up, and the
result was a smart and talented man.

But the mundane life was not for him. He just couldn't settle
down. He desired excitement, challenge, and adventure. He desired
the high life of beautiful women, free-flowing booze, and wild
travels. He could be considered a Don Quixote, looking for dragons
to slay and finding such in the world of the casinos.

Uston, a restless guy with a strong drive, read about blackjack
card counting and how to beat the casinos from Edward O. Thorp's
ground-breaking book *Beat the Dealer*, and that set him on the
road to becoming the most popular card counter in American lore.
Uston even developed his own counting systems that were actually

superior to Thorp's first attempts, although both Thorp's and Uston's counts were quite hard to play.

To this day, novice players emulate the Ken Uston persona—hard-drinking, high-rolling, constant whoring, along with dangerously and delightfully walking on that edge. One might characterize Uston as a man who created a "Ken Uston character" that he then played for the rest of his life, which would, unfortunately, not be all that long. Certainly his books are page-turners and worth a read by casino players. Uston was a far cry from the average casino player who trudges to the slot machines, plops down, and wastes away the hours. I guess it would be safe to say that Ken Uston was the anti-ploppy; he was the Zorro of blackjack play, the rogue.

While Uston's "big player" teams had tremendous success, the casinos finally caught on to the act, and Uston found himself banned from just about all Vegas properties, as well as properties around the world. He then went to wearing disguises, but these were often so poorly executed that casino personnel tended to recognize him immediately. Uston played in Atlantic City as well. My mentor, the Captain, ran into Uston at Resorts Casino and had this to say: "Everyone seemed to know who he was. He wore a poorly fitted wig, and the pit bosses were all around his table. I'm glad the guy didn't work for the CIA because we'd never be able to keep a secret."

When Uston was banned from playing in Atlantic City, he brought a lawsuit against the casinos that saw the New Jersey Supreme Court outlaw the barring of skilled blackjack players. Unlike Las Vegas, Nevada, the state of New Jersey was not controlled by the casino industry. The judges simply applied the Constitution to the situation and made their ruling: no more banning of skilled players. Card counters had become a protected class.

But the casinos did not take this ruling sitting down; the Atlantic City casinos made their games awful and generally not worth playing. They also began shuffling after every hand when they knew a skilled card counter was playing at a table. They limited the size of a card counter's bets. In short, the casinos acted like spoiled brats who were determined to get their way, and in fact they did. The Supreme Court of New Jersey had ruled one way; the casinos slithered out of the decision another way.

Uston died in Paris in 1987 at the age of 52. Conspiracy theorists believe he was murdered by a cabal of casino henchmen. The medical records show something quite different: he died of a heart attack, generally attributed to his heavy drinking and carousing lifestyle. Still, speculating that he was murdered has a romantic element that dying from a heart attack just can't match. That's probably why so many card counters believe that myth. If Ken Uston just fell over dead—*plunk!*—where is the glamour in that?

I am guessing that very few card counters don't know about Ken Uston. He became the mythological standard of the devil-may-care aggressive advantage player taking on the powerful casinos and beating them. He laid the groundwork for a generation of Ken Uston juniors, players who want to count cards, yes, but also players who want to count cards and live it up the way Uston did. Much of blackjack play for many players is more persona than anything else. It is closer to "I think I am Ken Uston, therefore I am."

* * *

I have been involved with some blackjack teams as a player and/or a financer. Some of my blackjack friends—James Diorio, Jerry "Stickman," Dom "the Dominator," Jodi Mention, Henry Tamburin, Manny Bronfman, Bill "Street Dog," Kyle Lansing, Donnie "the Duck," Kevin Thomason, and John Davis—have either been on these teams or at least know about them.

One team—the Lone Ranger team, as I now call it—was my most successful team and also my most troublesome. We played Atlantic City for six months in the late 1990s. This was at a time when the beautiful AP was suffering from a debilitating illness and couldn't come to the casinos with me.

The Lone Ranger team did not use the "big player" technique because, by this time, casinos were looking for that method. Instead, we had seven Lone Rangers who spread out to the various Atlantic City casinos that had decent games, mostly those found in the high-roller rooms. The rules in Atlantic City's high-roller rooms were quite favorable at that time, and if you could find a casino that dealt about 75 to 80 percent (or more) of the cards in a four- or six-deck shoe, the game could be beaten with alacrity. But playing shoe games, especially those six-deck shoes, took time; it also took patience because the counts in six-deck games are slow moving unlike the far more dynamic single- and double-deck games.

We played about six months of mostly weekends, as all of us had other jobs, and we were quite successful—at least in the money-making department. Our interpersonal skill set took quite a hit during this time. Friendships were broken, and most of us were disappointed in how some others of us behaved. Such a meltdown was not unique to our team; meltdowns occur with many teams. They almost seem par for the course.

You see, in team play not everyone is going to win every session or trip or even over somewhat extended periods of time. Some players will get their asses kicked day in and day out. Some will win far more than probability predicts, especially in the short runs, and team play for individual players is more or less the short run, though the team as a whole is playing many hands. The streaks, those lovely ups and devastating downs, are called variance—and variance can happen for good or ill for prolonged periods of time. We had a couple of players who were hotter than hot during this six-month period, we had a couple of players who won a decent amount, and we had three players who lost, one of whom lost a lot. The more decisions that a blackjack team plays, the better the chance it will be in the black. But individuals can be on the outer edges of the win/loss continuum during these periods of time. The team can be winning, maybe winning big, but individual players on those teams can be losing—perhaps losing big.

What starts to happen with the team is simple: those players who do really well are putting money into the pot—sometimes a lot of money—but those players who are losing, and especially those who are losing big, take money out of the pot—sometimes a lot of money. Resentment flourishes followed by suspicion. "Why is so-and-so losing so much? Maybe he can't play as well as we thought he could. Or, worse, is he actually keeping his wins for himself? Is the creep stealing from us?"

Once suspicion rears its ugly head, then come the accusations: "How come you're losing so much, huh? Are you stealing from the team?" Team play is almost religious in nature, requiring much faith, so the tendency is for the more fanatic, emotional, and hard-line players to get upset and aggressive toward those who aren't doing things the right way, meaning they aren't pulling their weight, meaning they aren't bringing in the money...meaning something fishy must be going on.

The reverse is also true. Losing players start to feel alienated and they might lash out at some of the other players because of the looks they give the loser when he reports still another losing day. So those who are winning a lot get angry and those who are losing a lot get angry, and the whole affair becomes quite unpleasant for everyone. Often it is a bad polygamous marriage.

Does this happen all the time? No. Some of the teams I dealt with had their emotional acts together. And some didn't. The Lone Rangers didn't. Still, that team won the silver bullets!

Interestingly enough, if you scratch any blackjack player and talk about team play, they will say they understand this situation and wouldn't fall into the trap themselves. Maybe this is true, but some of the individuals who went Looney Tunes on a couple of my teams proclaimed before they joined the team that they would never get upset because they understood the roll of variance even in games where the player has the edge. Famous *first* words.

I like to compare team play to investing in the stock market. Your broker asks you if you can handle risk. You say risk doesn't bother you, so go for those dynamic high-risk investments. Suddenly those investments tank and lose you a load of money, and you are *not* cool and calm. No, no, no, you are completely, totally devastated because your mouth was able to say you can handle risk, but your emotional equipment went haywire when that risk turned out to whack you over the head with big losses.

I am a believer in Hamlet's response to Polonius when Polonius asked him what he was reading. Hamlet said, "Words, words, words." You will never know how a person will react, despite whatever "words, words, words" he utters. Actions certainly do speak louder than words, and that is a good warning for those of you who are flirting with team play. Be careful, because those "words, words, words" will often give themselves the lie.

One of my recent team-playing experiences took place over four days in Tunica, Mississippi, a couple of years before I was banned from all the casinos in that state. Michael Kaplan, who had done an article about me for *Harper's* magazine, wanted to do an article about Joanna W., who had appeared on the short-lived television show *Ultimate Blackjack Tour*. The article was for the January 2006 issue of *Glamour*. Joanna W. had been a player on a Russian blackjack team that had hit Vegas rather hard the previous year. She is said to have won $80,000. Not a bad take.

Kaplan wanted to know if Joanna could join my Tunica team and display her blackjack talents to him in the casinos. One of Joanna's talents seemed to be costuming—creating different characters based on how she looked—in order to fool the pit. If her costuming were as bad as Uston's, our team could lose one of its players fairly quickly. Most people who do costuming are a far cry from the professional people who do costuming for movies and theater.

Although she was presented to us as a cunning card counter with true skills and great wins, Joanna had a small problem: our team would have to finance her because she was short of money. I don't know why some card-counting blackjack players (and some poker players, too) can't hold on to their hard-won money, but some of them either spend, spend, spend or go from their advantage-play games into other games that they just can't beat. I have seen some great poker players play craps as if they were just released from an asylum, making bad bets left and right and betting up their bankrolls like crazy. I've seen card counters do the exact same things. They should memorize the following:

- Never play a game that you can't beat or

- Only bet small if you feel you must play a game you can't beat because you are looking to have fun.

I will readily admit that advantage play is not fun—at least not for me. I find that it is work; it is a grind. I find the casino environment to be a noisy place in which I have to work to make some dough. I've never fallen into the Ken Uston mythology. I know the score. To me an exciting evening is not being in a casino but sitting by my fireplace, drink in hand, kissing my wife, the beautiful AP, and asking her if we can get rid of our loud parrot. (No, no, I like our parrot; I just say this to get a rise out of her, since the parrot thinks she will be the first actual reader of this book. Honey, I love our parrot.)

Still, why not let Joanna W. play on our team? Adding another good player, a player who had played with a great group of card counters, could only help us, even if we had to finance her. We all assumed she was a good player, and indeed she was.

She would be joining four of us—Dom "the Dominator," Jerry "Stickman," Bill "Street Dog," and me—who were instructors in the Golden Touch dice control and blackjack classes, and this would give us great publicity for our classes, since we all assumed our Golden Touch team would also be highlighted in Kaplan's piece. It wasn't to be.

As Dominator wrote in an email to me, "After reading the article, I remember what really pissed me off—he never mentioned us in the article! It was all about her and never what happened to us in Tunica. We thought because she didn't win enough money and we won most of it, he shied away from writing about that. If you remember, we had to come up with all the money for the team,

$15 to $100, this was a decent take. Making $4,605 over three days came to $921 per person or $307 per day. Not bad at all. Had the four of us been playing our normal stakes, which were much higher, the wins would have been much higher as well.

So how did Joanna W. do with her costuming? According to Michael Kaplan, she was great. Joanna was a pretty young woman to begin with, and she played a nurse, a prostitute, a drunk, a librarian type, and a Southern belle during her various gaming sessions. I've no doubt she did a great job, though I think Kaplan might have been somewhat dazzled by this young lady's looks and energy. Dynamic card counters, both male and female, have a certain appeal to the lay public, who really have no idea of the grind it all is.

The fact that none of the Golden Touch members were mentioned in the article is just the way things go. Writers pick and choose what they want to highlight, and so did Kaplan. From my experiences with him, he seemed a nice enough fellow. I have no idea what happened to Joanna W.

That team play in Tunica came at a time when Tunica still had great single- and double-deck games. After that year, the blackjack games deteriorated as they have deteriorated in Atlantic City and Las Vegas. It takes a little more effort and circumspection to choose and play today's games. Winning is quite game-dependent.

Card counters and shuffle trackers can still get the edge over the house, but they must find the right games to play. While all men might be created equal, all blackjack games are not.

CHAPTER 10

The Working Man

It would be impossible to go through an almost quarter century of stories about card counting and advantage play. First, I can't remember everything. Second, most of the days were routine. Although I do have some phenomenal stories that I will relate (phenomenal in my opinion), keep in mind that playing as often as I did in as many casinos as I did with the success that I had would tend to generate certain events that in retrospect might sound as if they were everyday occurrences. Not so. Card counting was routine. The days were mostly routine.

Let me give you an overview of a typical day, a typical week, of play for us.

My stays in Vegas tended to be three weeks long. I'd head out there two or three times in the summers and most major vacations, such as Christmas, winter break, and Easter, and these would be weeklong trips. And I would go to Atlantic City for two- and three-day trips every other weekend. I certainly did put in a lot of time. In the 1990s just about all of my trips were with the beautiful AP. After Michael, our youngest son, graduated from college, the beautiful AP made her announcement: "I am now retired. I don't ever want to play in another casino again. Greg and Mike are out of college, and I don't have to go in those places again." She has stuck to her word. The few times she has come with me to casinos since were occasions to meet friends for dinner or see a show.

I never pushed my play into the realm of the ridiculous. I kept my own pace. The Captain always believed that a good player had to impose his own rhythm on the casinos and not allow the casinos' 24/7 adrenaline-soaked rhythm to influence him. Certainly easier said than done for most players. Just look around a casino and you can see that it is as though everyone has been given a massive dose of methamphetamine. The casinos are pumping in the speed, and the players are pumping out their money.

Such pumping is great for the casinos and bad for the players because it makes the players play longer, and the longer the players play, the better the chance that the casino edge will be hacking away at them. Drinking is a helpful drug for casinos, too. They just pour it in glasses and the players drain the stuff into their mouths. I sometimes think as a cost-cutting measure, casinos could just hook up their players to an alcohol IV and save the expense of glasses and cocktail waitresses. Here is a saying I always liked: "Get high, and your bankroll will die." Okay, it isn't too poetic, but it gets the point across. Gamblers are just a herd of cattle to the casinos; gamblers exist to be skinned, and their bankrolls exist to be devoured.

Except for that one week when I lost my mind in Atlantic City, I never fell for the casino hype ever again. Certainly I enjoy a couple drinks, but my days never had an alcohol content attached to them. Maybe at dinner I would have a glass (or two) of wine, but more often than not I wouldn't play at night because the conditions were too crowded.

Casinos rope you in other ways, too. I kid you not, there is even a casino smell—somewhat reduced nowadays because people don't smoke as much—which consists of adrenaline, smoke, booze, noise (yes, casino noise has a smell to it), sweat, and massive doses of hope. When I walked into casinos I could smell the scent of players playing. That scent could send many gamblers into tizzies, but for me it was the smell of work.

Our typical day would begin around 5:00 or 5:30 with a long workout. If we were staying on the Strip, we'd walk from one end to the other. Let me take what had been one of my favorite casinos, Treasure Island, and go from there.

The beautiful AP and I would walk all the way to the Hacienda, which was demolished in 1996 (Mandalay Bay was built there), then walk all the way back, past Treasure Island to Vegas World, which closed in 1995 (the property then became the Stratosphere), and we'd turn around and go back to Treasure Island. We'd take showers, have breakfast, then go out to play. I rarely played Treasure Island during the day. I preferred to hit other casinos. I did violate one of my normal rules for Treasure Island: I played at night in the high-roller room, which was rarely crowded. For a long stretch of time, Treasure Island was my favorite place to play. I felt it was my own, personal Treasure Island.

We had some interesting experiences during these long morning walks. One morning I was regaling the beautiful AP about my sharp observations of everything around me because I am a perceptive writer.

"You see, my beauty, I notice everything around me. I'm a writer. I observe everything. No knock on you, but you don't really observe anywhere near as much as I do. I observe it all, and that's why I'm a good writer. I have a writer's senses. I observe."

She nodded and asked, "You observed that, right?"

"What?"

"The girl on a leash, wearing a dog collar," she said.

"What?"

"Right behind us," she said.

I turned around, and there they were—the guy had the heavily tattooed girl, who was in a studded dog collar, on a leash. They were walking the opposite direction, and she was walking ahead of him as if she were a dog.

"While you were explaining how observant you are, how you observe everything because you are a writer, they walked right past us."

On another walk, we almost got mugged by several creeps not far from Vegas World. We were staying at the former Sahara (you had to have a renovated room because the old rooms were disgusting), and we decided to walk downtown and back. These were really our early Vegas days because we didn't realize that the area between Vegas World—which was perpendicular across the street from Sahara—and downtown was a seedy part of the Strip, much as Atlantic City was seedy. Except for walks on the Boardwalk, you stayed out of the neighborhoods there.

So off we went, and here is what made that walk memorable. During that time in our lives, the beautiful AP was making our clothes—mostly shirts for me, blouses for her, and also some vests for me. She had made two matching shirts for us for that trip—quite beautiful, too—and we wore those for our walk that day. We looked like two dopey tourists, two bumpkins in our matching shirts. Since it was so early in the morning, only the remnants of scum were left on the streets, but there was quite a bit of automobile traffic.

As we were about five blocks away from Vegas World heading downtown, several "gentlemen" started heading toward us. Growing up in New York City does teach you several things about criminals. First, they tend to look like criminals; they rarely look like bankers. (Okay some bankers *are* criminals who look like bankers, but they aren't mugging you on the street.) Thus, looks in these cases are rarely deceiving. Second, you never ignore them; you must look them right in the face. Criminals aren't going away if you ignore them. Looking right at them sometimes causes them to figure you aren't afraid or maybe you have a gun. Other times it has no effect. If it has no good effect, then you run or yell or fight or do whatever the hell you have to do to protect yourself. Yes, the fight-or-flight response kicks in fast.

"When I squeeze your arm, we run right across Vegas Boulevard," I said to AP. My plan was to have the traffic come between us and them. When I saw the cars approaching, I squeezed her arm, and we ran like maniacs across Las Vegas Boulevard, and the cars came between us and them—and "them" were running at us. They didn't look too happy when dozens of speeding cars stopped them from getting to us. We then ran as fast as we could back to the Sahara, and that was the last time we ever decided to walk to downtown Vegas. That was one Vegas gamble we just would not take.

On one solitary walk one morning I decided to walk over the faux Brooklyn Bridge at New York, New York. I have walked over the real Brooklyn Bridge maybe 100 times. On the New York, New York one, I was greeted by a host of prostitutes who were selling their wares—at 5:00 AM! I didn't buy anything and scurried through them as fast as I could. I have never really understood why men go to prostitutes. I always think when I see one, *What the hell does she have crawling around in her?* Men, if you think this way, you'll save yourself a lot of pain, medical bills, and money. Disease is not something that stays in Vegas or Atlantic City or anywhere else, for that matter. It follows you home.

After our morning play, we'd head back to the hotel, take a nap, then have some lunch, and head out again to another casino for some afternoon play. It was usually these afternoon sessions where we would meet up with some of our friends. We didn't necessarily make arrangements to meet, but we all tended to follow the better games and thus all tended to go to the same casinos.

If we were staying downtown or at local casino hotels such as Sunset Station (another favorite of mine) or in non-casino hotels (which we often did), we'd usually work out in the hotel's spa. Even as I gained 100 pounds over my quarter-century casino career, I always worked out. I still do. Only now I don't really need to lift weights, because lifting me has become more than enough.

I tended to stay at non-casino hotels quite often. That gave me the run of the city, and never did I have to worry about some casino boss getting the wonderful idea of locking me out of my "big shot" comped room. I also preferred staying in casino-hotels where I did not play because their games were not good. In Vegas midweek and in Atlantic City in winter you can get some really low prices.

At times I did violate these protocols. I loved staying and being comped as if I were a big shot (truthfully a stupid thing to be) at many casinos in Las Vegas such as Treasure Island, Bellagio, Mandalay Bay, Monte Carlo, Golden Nugget, Desert Inn, Rio, Sunset Station, and Marriot/Rampart. Playing the role of big shot didn't always protect me from being banned or worse; in fact, being a big shot probably caused me more trouble than it was worth.

In Atlantic City I liked being a big shot at Taj Mahal, Bally's, Bally's Grand (now ACH), Showboat, Tropicana (when it was Trop-world), and the Marina (now Golden Nugget).

I am human, and being picked up in limos, given delicious gourmet meals and great comped shows, and having hosts cater to me were great temptations. At times I fell into the very traps I warn gamblers about. Yes, I did beat these casinos, but I think I often gave them too much of a look at how I played. And the more the casino bosses see of you, the more they learn about what you are actually doing. That is not good.

The afternoon play could be at several casinos. I tried (but sometimes failed) to spread my play around town so that no casino got a good bead on me (except for the ones where I was acting Mr. Big Shot). I think my weakness was a typical one for advantage players: I tended to get greedy. If a casino had a good game, I sometimes stayed too long at the party. I did this with both blackjack and dice control—it was and still is my fatal flaw. At my best, I gave myself a half hour to a maximum of 45 minutes (maybe an hour) to play in one casino, then I walked. In Vegas, with so many casinos, I had plenty to choose from and no reason to stay at any one for too long a period of time. I do believe that playing short sessions is one of the main keys for not getting on the radar of given casinos. Today there are not as many good games, so your opportunities are much more limited.

The Atlantic City trips merely substituted the Strip with the Boardwalk for our walk—one end of the Boardwalk to the other end, or we'd do spa workouts in bad weather. As I said, we stayed off the streets in Atlantic City, but on the Boardwalk there were enough cops to make us feel safe.

I didn't worry about spreading my play around in Atlantic City as I did in Vegas. Since Atlantic City couldn't ban me, that was one thing in my favor. Also, many of my weekends were spent with the Captain and his crew of high rollers, and it would be stupid for a casino to harass a member of that group, because most of them were wild gamblers who lost far more than I could ever make even if I got ridiculously lucky for a ridiculously long period of time—like the rest of my life. Even betting black chips and the occasional purple as I did by the turn of the new century, the members of the Captain's crew were betting and losing stacks of orange for a few decades. (Although true that a casino would be nuts to go after anyone involved with the Captain, Tropworld—now Tropicana—did so. It went after the Captain, the Arm, and Jimmy P. in a big way. I'll tell that story in *I Am A Dice Controller*.)

Tunica's gambling landscape was also pretty easy to navigate— at least for 10 years until Harrah's took control of the major proper-ties. I played at just about every casino in the venue. I rarely stayed at most of the hotels. I preferred staying at Horseshoe or the Grand (now Harrah's). Whatever troubles I had in Tunica were caused by dice control, not card counting. The casino bosses actually knew me because I did a radio show in Memphis that was sponsored by the casinos. I was the weekly expert—and for most of my Tunica career that had some impact—until Harrah's took over.

I did play in the Midwest, but I rarely had long stays in those casinos. Midwestern casinos are not in close proximity to each other. Going from one casino to the next took up too much time. So my Midwest play was limited.

Having heard horror stories from other card counters about playing in foreign lands, including Native American casinos, which are for all intents and purposes their own nations, I stayed clear of such play as much as possible. But I did violate my rule about no Native American casino play when I did my Frank Scoblete's Gamblers' Jamboree, a series of instructional seminars and lectures, in Albuquerque, New Mexico, at the Isleta Casino, a casino where my friend Clyde Callicott was director of marketing. Clyde and I both did the radio show from Memphis for many years together until he left over a salary dispute. He was a funny, intelligent, smart conversationalist, and the show's quality dipped quite a bit when he left.

I played for about a week that fall in Albuquerque. I played in Canada a few times, but overall my play was essentially limited to American casinos.

I had a general rule about my longer trips. I didn't play on my first day in town or my last day in town (though my last day was usually a few hours before an early morning flight). On the first day, my flight from New York to Vegas was about five and a half hours. Throw in an hour or two at Kennedy Airport and then about a half hour to an hour getting my bags and getting to the hotel after I landed in Vegas, and that's the equivalent of a working day. So I refrained from playing because air travel is tiring.

On the last day, I just took my results and what would be, would be. I always felt that playing on the last day made me feel more like a gambler, meaning I couldn't get enough of the games. I preferred to be cool in the face of my desire to continue to play—cool so I knew I had the control of my play, not following the pumping, throbbing rhythms of the casino. I wanted total control of myself.

My last-day dictum flies in the face of the math of advantage play, and many card counters think I am wrong about this. Certainly, the more decisions you play, the better the chance that you will be ahead. The math here is clearly against me. But emotions work, too. I wanted absolute control of myself. Going off the edge when

I was in Atlantic City that second trip made me totally aware of the fact that even skilled players can lose their minds. I wanted to control myself completely. What better way than by resisting the urge to continue? I thought of that last day as overtime. As a worker I didn't need overtime. I was making enough in the time I gave myself between the second day and the second-to-last day.

I also knew I would be going to a casino within a week—probably Atlantic City or Tunica—so not playing on a last day wasn't such a big deal to me. I have continued with that philosophy right up until today. I think it has stood me in good stead.

CHAPTER 11

Glory Days / Gory Days

Okay, card counting and other advantage-play methods are work, but I will admit that it was fun because of what it told me about myself. I had a certain sense of—*this is going to sound insane*—glory doing what I did. The casino industry is predacious, exploiting the weaknesses of people in order to take their money. They are lionesses looking to pick off the weakest of the herd so they can devour them.

Most casino gamblers, indeed the overwhelming majority of casino gamblers, are the weakest, slowest-running creatures in the herd. The bosses know exactly what they are doing in order to nail these folks. Just look at the percentages of income casinos make, and you'll see that players are playing games that they can't beat often for amounts of money better spent elsewhere.

A few of us, a tiny fraction of a percentage, manage to beat them by turning the contest in our favor. Some card counters have beaten the casinos for millions; some like Paul Keen have beaten them for far, far less than a million, but the fact remains that there are players out there that can beat the house. There is a certain glory in that; at least I think so.

Of course, with a war comes casualties, and there are many sessions where the advantage player gets his ass kicked—the lioness takes some chunks out of his hide. Those sessions do not bring any glory; they are merely gory interludes between wins. All of this is, sadly, par for the course. You are going to get bloodied. Expect it. And you are going to react when you get bitten by the casino predator—at least I react. I never feel good after a defeat, never. Even saying to myself "I played the best I could play" is like the fighter saying "I fought the best I could fight" as he's being taken to the emergency room after being knocked out.

Still, a skilled card counter can win over time, and to achieve that skill you do not have to be a genius. You just have to work at it. While there are plenty of times when the card counter is severely bloodied, there are many times when he rips away at the flesh of the casino lioness, bloodying her even worse. It's certainly a close contest, but it is a close contest that the card counter wins if he plays his cards right.

My Sunken Treasure at Treasure Island

One of my favorite casinos was Treasure Island (now also called TI). I used to go there all the time, even for a week or more. I loved playing in the high-roller room because in most of my sessions I was either the only player or one of two.

I made it a point to play with the "female pit folks" because they were professional and friendly—they also liked the boxes of candy that I brought with me to almost every session. I made sure that two boxes were always open so they could snatch a candy or two (or three or four) as I was playing. The more candy they ate, the less they analyzed my play. Even the dealers took some candy as they went on their breaks. We all got along famously. Treasure Island had a wonderful double-deck game with great penetration and great rules. As I've said, I felt that Treasure Island was my own personal Treasure Island. Over time my edge certainly did play out.

However, I had my most devastating loss at this casino—a $12,000 beating that took place over a single hour, *one single hour*. The counts got high time after time, but I just couldn't win more than a single hand in a row—but I could lose several in a row. Those several often tended to be my highest bets in high positive counts. Even in positive counts, the game is close enough to give you ulcer-inducing losses.

Needless to say, unlike the cold-blooded card counters of literature and websites, I was shaken. I took my remaining chips off the table and started to head for the cage, which was in the front area of the casino. Before I left the high-roller room, one of the floor women stopped me and asked me, "Frank, do you want a candy?" She was not being sarcastic; she liked me and felt sorry that I had been devoured by Lady Luck (variance, in scientific terms) and spit out into a bloody heap. I took the candy and ate it, but I couldn't taste it. I had a dry mouth and a tormented soul.

In my room I lay in bed curled in the fetal position and I would have sucked my thumb had I not kept telling myself, "Remember, you are an adult. You are an adult." Maybe other card counters have experienced the same feelings of defeat, depression, and despondency after monstrous losses. I don't know. But I do know that I have never lost the ability to feel like crap after losing. Such losses do not stop me from playing; they just feel awful. I take a break, think about sucking my thumb, and then go back for another session later that day, or another day, another month. I am like a fighter who got knocked down, but I will get up. I've always gotten up.

It took me a week to make back that money—I had to grind away, session after session, day after day. I never had a really hot run. As I said, I had to grind away. It ain't easy sometimes.

The Renzey Rout at Treasure Island

A fellow writer friend of mine, Fred Renzey, author of two excellent books—*Blackjack Bluebook II* and *77 Ways to Get the Edge at Casino Poker*—was the first card counter I ever saw banned from Treasure Island.

Renzey created many twists in basic strategy that have never (or rarely) been thought of. I have to say he is one of those guys who can play blackjack for relatively high stakes and also understand the mathematics—he knows the math of the game as well as anyone I have met.

We were playing near the main entrance of the Treasure Island casino, not far from the cage. The high-roller room was crowded on that particular night, so we decided to play at the lower-stakes tables. The fact that tables allow lower stakes does not mean you can't bet your normal amounts. In the high-roller room, the minimum bet could be $100, and the maximum bet could be $5,000. On a lower-stakes table, the minimum bet could be $25 with a maximum of $2,000. You could still use $100 as your minimum bet and $500 or $600 as your maximum bet if that were your normal spread. (The maximums can be more or less than the figures I just gave. Each casino, perhaps each shift, can follow different practices. During the day the stakes are usually lower than they are in the evening.)

Renzey and I sat at different tables. It's usually not a good practice to have two players at the same table—the *only* two players—counting cards (I have violated this rule quite often). It becomes fairly obvious fairly soon that both of you are counting, because the bets tend to reflect each other. But I could see Renzey's bets and I could see he was using an extremely aggressive spread. I wondered if I had made a mistake in telling him that Treasure Island didn't seem to mind players who spread their bets. I should have said *conservatively* spread their bets.

It was too late for me to tell him that the pit boss had come into the pit to watch his play. I didn't want to be associated with him in the pit boss' mind. I also didn't want to feed him to the wolves, so I made various facial expressions to tell him to get up and leave. I contorted my face so much that the dealer said, "Sir, are you all right? Do you need help?"

The beautiful AP and I had a simple saying that we lived by when playing blackjack: "There's no such thing as paranoia." If we felt the pit was observing us too closely, if we even had a hint of such a thing, we got the hell out of the game and out of the casino. But no one was bothering to look at me as I was keeping my spread at one-to-four or one-to-five. One key to bet-spreading is not to jump too fast. Let us say you are betting $100 as your minimum. The count goes up. It's best to just double your bet. If the count continues to go up and you win a hand, then you can let your $200 bet and the $200 win ride. If you lose the hand, you can put up $300 and make it look as if you are playing some kind of martingale. There are many ways to cover your betting tracks.

Renzey evidently wasn't doing that. He was hopping, skipping, and jumping. Within a few minutes the pit boss pushed Renzey's bet back to him, told him he wasn't welcome to play blackjack in the casino but that he could play other games, and that was that for that session. Renzey got up and left. I got up about 10 minutes later and met him outside to head for another casino.

My Pal Henry Tamburin: Genius and Drooling Idiot

One of my best friends in the gambling world is best-selling author and columnist Henry Tamburin. Henry wrote the *Take the Money and Run* series of books and he is also a columnist for the best magazines in the business. I have played blackjack and craps with Henry too many times to count over more than two decades.

Henry is an excellent card counter and he has some fun ways to prevent the casino from knowing what he's up to. He bores the floor person to death with pictures of his kids, his grandkids, his house, his car, his wife, and people he worked with when he was in chemical engineering (oh, yes, the hardest of chemistry degrees is a doctorate in chemical engineering, which Henry has) and discussions of what he likes to eat, how to cook various nauseating food stuff, how he is landscaping his garden, what new things he's bought for his house, his medical woes (mostly made up), etc. He tells sleep-inducing stories that never end. He can count cards and discuss the intricacies of something you have no interest in, the details of which cause your eyes to glaze over, the length and breadth of which can kill you.

Floor people and pit bosses flee him after a short while and rarely come back to his table. He then counts cards without concern that anyone will care what he's doing. Henry Tamburin is a blackjack plague, the blackjack zombie apocalypse. I swear I have seen drool coming down his chin. Such a brilliant man transforming himself into a dope, a total bore, an idiot, is an amazing talent that few human beings, including our finest actors, could achieve.

One night while Henry was boring the hell out of everyone around us, he had the pleasure of seeing my greatest losing streak, which took place at Fitzgerald's casino in Tunica, Mississippi. Dominator was also at that particular table and—hold on to your heart muscles—I lost 22 hands in a row. I did not lose anywhere near $12,000 as I had at Treasure Island, because many of those bets were for minimums, but still, 22 losing hands in succession is quite an event. Prior to that my greatest consecutive losing streak was 14. (How do I keep track of my losing runs? Simple. After I lose four or five hands in a row—something you can figure without actually keeping a count—I then start to count the losses. It is not something I enjoy doing; it's just part of my makeup. As a baseball player I was always concerned about my statistics and I guess this is a carryover.)

Henry has been with me through thick and thin—he was there when I went through the worst "getting banned from casinos week," which I will write about in *I Am a Dice Controller*. We have operated a seminar business together. His publishing company has published two of my books, and I consider him one hell of a guy. We've done seminars, classes, and gamblers' jamborees together. He's a fabulous, fascinating speaker—unlike the character he creates at a blackjack table. He's also a great teacher. He is someone who can do and can teach, too. Keep in mind he is *Dr.* Henry Tamburin, and his degree is in one of the toughest, if not the toughest, disciplines imaginable.

Henry Tamburin is a *were*-idiot (the were is pronounced as it is in *werewolf*); in real life he is a brilliant man, but when the full blackjack moon rises into the night, he transforms into a grating and painful creature. Like the werewolf under a full moon, Henry howls his delight as he wins boatloads of chips and bores everyone around him to death.

Stanford Wong Creates the Blackjack Bible

One of my favorite gambling authorities for the past quarter century has been Stanford Wong. His book *Professional Blackjack* had the most influence over my learning and my play. I think Wong has influenced more blackjack players than any single authority.

I never got to see Wong play, but I did meet him when he took a course on dice control with me. Wong had always been skeptical that players could control the dice, so I offered him the opportunity to take my two-day class, which was given by Golden Touch Craps. To think that the advantage player and author who had the profoundest effect on me had become *my* student boggled my mind.

My dice-control partner at the time was the Dominator, and he and I had lunch several times with Wong during this period of time. I was somewhat like a groupie, asking him questions one after the other. I am not a person who asks for autographs (though I love to give them, so if I ever meet you, please ask me for an autograph), but I was "this close" to asking him for one. That says something. I once sat next to Muhammad Ali at a fight; I talked to Ali, but I never asked him for his autograph.

I kind of did a mini-interview with Wong and found what he had to say quite interesting. Of course, I forgot some of the interview, so I emailed him recently and asked if he would answer some questions—probably the same questions I had asked him when we had lunch together.

FRANK: When did you first get interested in casino gambling and advantage play?

STANFORD WONG: I have always been very competitive. As a child I learned that being overly competitive was not a good way to keep friends. So I was happy to learn about casino games because they allowed me to be as competitive as I wanted to be.

[Wong's competitive nature reminds me of my own. I was an avid athlete as a kid, playing basketball and baseball. I belonged to one basketball team that went 55–0. I wrote about that one in my book *Confessions of a Wayward Catholic*. I belonged to one that went to the final New York City Championship Game when I was a student at St. John's Prep. We lost that one, ending our undefeated record. I would play on several baseball teams each summer. In college I boxed, which was the stupidest thing I ever did in my life, and I am paying for it now. That story is in *The Virgin Kiss*.]

FRANK: Anyone inspire you to learn advantage play?

STANFORD WONG: Not really. I gravitated toward advantage play on my own. Ed Thorp's *Beat the Dealer* was the first advantage-play book that I read, but I had already done considerable analyzing of blackjack on an office calculator before Thorp wrote his book.

FRANK: What games can you play with an edge?

STANFORD WONG: I have analyzed many games, figured out how to get an edge, wrote it up in a book, and then moved on to another game. The only game that I have won a considerable amount of money at is blackjack. There are several other games that I have learned how to play with an edge but have not actually made much money at: video poker, Pai Gow poker, casino games tournaments, craps, and sports betting.

FRANK: What kind of betting do you do at these games?

STANFORD WONG: I bet big enough to make the games interesting to me but small enough to fly under casino radar. Generally my big bets are less than $1,000.

FRANK: What were your learning curves?

STANFORD WONG: The first game I learned how to beat was black-jack. It took me a couple of months to get proficient enough with Thorp's 10-count to take on the casinos of Nevada, but I was a full-time engineering student and a couple of months shy of 21 when I started to learn the 10-count. Had I wanted to learn it faster, I could have. For most casinos games that I learned to beat, what took me the most time was developing strategies rather than learning to apply them. Learning to toss dice until I could generate more primary hits than double pitches was the most time-consuming skill I learned, taking months of part-time practice.

FRANK: How did you go about becoming the "you" you are now?

STANFORD WONG: I drifted into it. I never intended to become a professional gambler or a publisher. Before I wrote my first book, my intention was to be a college professor. To that end I earned a PhD from Stanford University. My wife accepted a job in La Jolla, California, so we moved there. I applied for teaching positions at San Diego State University and the University of San Diego, and both wanted to hire me, but neither of them could figure out a way to pay me. So I played blackjack and published books while waiting for the financial situations of the local universities to improve. I enjoyed working for myself, so what started out as a temporary use of my time turned out to be permanent.

FRANK: Did you have any trouble with barrings or bannings? [Barring is usually the casino telling you that you can't play blackjack but you can play other games. Banning usually means that the casino tells you not to come back.]

STANFORD WONG: I have been barred from only a dozen casinos. I could easily have been barred at many more because casino management has pictures of me, but I have taken steps to minimize barrings. The bigger a customer bets, the higher the level of management that is notified of that customer's presence, so I keep my bets small enough that my presence does not get passed up to the high-level people who are likely to recognize me. I patronize many casinos, instead of concentrating on only the few with the best games.

None of my barrings was harsh. The worst barrings I have had involved getting kicked out of comped hotel rooms late in the evening. I was able to find other accommodations in all those instances.

FRANK: Any adventures you think are exciting, funny, harrowing, or cautionary?

STANFORD WONG: I did have one trip that can be considered cautionary. I flew to Macau to take advantage of what at that time was a fabulous blackjack game. The rules were so good that basic strategy gave the player an edge of more than 0.2 percent right after a shuffle. Yet I lost, day after day. The biggest bet controlled the play of the hand, so I had to be making the biggest bet on every hand I played, lest another player make a bad play involving my bet. When my trip bankroll shrank to the point where I could no longer make the biggest bets on my hands, I flew home. I think I was getting an honest game because I had big winning trips to Macau both before and after the bad trip. The lesson to be learned is to be sure to have access to enough money to be able to weather a huge unlucky spell.

FRANK: What advice would you give players about advantage play or any play, for that matter?

STANFORD WONG: My advice is to keep advantage play part-time. Do something else with the major part of your time, something more valuable to society. You will find that more satisfying than becoming a full-time advantage player.

John Gollehon and Marvin Karlins at Atlantic City's Tropicana

Author John Gollehon has written more than 20 books on casino gambling. You probably can find his books in airport bookstores throughout the country—and that is a coup for any writer, as airport bookstores do great business. I am guessing just about anyone who reads gambling books has read one, two, or 300 of his. He is also a noted publisher whose company has been responsible for bringing some excellent writers to the fore.

Marvin Karlins is another prodigiously productive author, having also written more than 20 books, some about gambling, some about individuals and events, some about non-gambling topics, and even some fiction. (I really enjoyed his novel, *The Grey Avengers*.) The guy is quite intelligent and quite talented. He is also a psychologist. I can't remember how Karlins and I made each other's acquaintance, but we set up a meeting at Tropworld (Tropicana) casino in Atlantic City. We'd have dinner, talk, and maybe play at the tables together.

When I met Marvin outside the restaurant at Tropworld, he was with another fellow—one of his publishers, none other than John Gollehon. This would be a two-for-one dinner from my perspective! I had read some of Gollehon's books and I had read a couple by Karlins by that time and I was excited to meet them both.

I don't know if other writers have the same feelings that I do—I love to meet people who have been able to write an entire book, get it published, and actually find a readership. I *really* love to meet writers who have written several or many books because I know the discipline that must go into producing more than one book. Give writing books a try, and you'll see it is not that easy. Writers who have reached the top of the list—as had Karlins and Gollehon—actually put me in awe. And I was about to have dinner with them.

Karlins seemed to be a happy guy and he had great enthusiasm for gambling. He told me as we sat down to dinner, "I love to play, sometimes too much." Though he was not a card counter, he was a knowledgeable player. His game was craps, but he was not a dice controller; he used a weird sort of martingale as his betting method. Needless to say, he was not a long-term winner when I met him.

Gollehon, on the other hand, was a total grouch—at least he started off the evening grouching away. He complained about everything—the restaurant, the food, the waiters, the lighting, the small print of the menu, other writers. His surliness knew no bounds. I thought it was going to be an endless evening.

Once dinner with Karlins and Gollehon was over and we were walking through the casino, I found out what was troubling Gollehon—he had an illness called diverticulitis and he was having a flare-up. Trust me, I know about these types of diseases—the beautiful AP suffered from ulcerative colitis—and when he said, "I'm sorry. Overlook what I've been saying. I'm in pain," I quickly dropped my original opinion of him as a grumpy complainer and realized his biggest complaint had to do with nature and genetics, which had bestowed upon him lengthy periods of agony.

So as we walked through the casino checking out the games, I never told them that the Captain came to that casino with his crew. Karlins knew about the Captain and seemed interested in meeting him. That could have occurred at Tropworld if the Captain had happened to be there. Unfortunately, he wasn't.

An interesting phenomenon exists that I have seen in many advantage players and many gambling authors, though I have not seen this in the general casino-player population—they have little love for the casinos. Indeed, many authors and advantage players have a strong dislike of the industry. Neither Gollehon nor Karlins seemed in love with casinos, though both seemed to enjoy playing the games.

While I did not get to see either of these two writers play blackjack, I can safely use them as examples of smart players who know the math and the score of casino games—that score, sans advantage play, being that players must ultimately lose. Gollehon seemed to take this more seriously than Karlins, who seemed to enjoy somewhat wild betting at craps. Gollehon seemed somewhat more conservative. But both knew what the essence of the casino world was all about—the casinos winning, the players losing.

Celebrity Blackjack Camouflage

In my book *Beat Blackjack Now!: The Easiest Way to Get the Edge!*
I discuss a type of advantage play using celebrities as interference.
I first learned this technique at Sunset Station in Vegas. Famous
actor Tony Curtis and his wife would come into the casino to play.
Curtis made scores of movies, I think the greatest of which might
be *Some Like It Hot*, co-starring Marilyn Monroe and Jack Lemon.
This may be the funniest film ever made, and the more I see it
the more I love it.

I noticed that whenever Curtis came into the casino, all eyes
were on him. If he sat down to play blackjack, then again all eyes
were on him. By chance I got to sit at the same table with him one
afternoon, and as I was counting, all eyes were on Tony Curtis. No
one—not the other players, not the dealer, not the fans walking
by the table, not the floor person, not the pit boss, not the casino
manager who dropped by—looked at me or my play. I was pushing
my bet spread on a double-deck game all the way from 1 to 10! In
any other situation, I would have been barred as Fred Renzey was
barred at Treasure Island. But no one even noticed I was there.
Thank you, Tony Curtis.

Since my bankroll has been large enough to play high enough
stakes to allow me high-roller-room status, I have been able to play
at the same tables or in the same high-roller rooms with famous
professional basketball players—one who might be considered the
greatest of all time—some famous actors and several pretty actresses
(one of whom still has a popular television show), a bunch of
wrestlers from the WWF (before it became the WWE), some famous
baseball players, and some very famous boxers in several divisions,
including a heavyweight champion. I also played at the same tables
with "The Godfather of Soul," James Brown, on many occasions. He
sweated as much playing blackjack as he did when he performed.
When you are at a table or in the same room as celebrities, just
remember what Emily Dickinson wrote: "I'm nobody." You want

to be nobody when you can beat the house, and those celebrities allow you to enjoy nobodyness.

(Note I have not mentioned who the living ones are since I gravitated to them when I saw them. No reason to give away my talented cohorts or maybe screw up their play. By the way, sometimes some celebrities enjoyed being a part of my ruse and were very helpful. Some celebrities were actually fans of mine, and that can be mind-blowing.)

The Ears Have It

This date is ingrained in my mind: June 28, 1997. It was the date of the famous Tyson "Bite Fight," where an enraged Mike Tyson bit both ears of heavyweight champion Evander "the Real Deal" Holyfield. The Bite Fight was their second meeting within a year. Their first fight saw Holyfield beat the living daylights out of Tyson, ending the fight with a TKO in round 11.

Somewhere in round three with Tyson perhaps realizing he could not intimidate or beat the powerful Holyfield, he chomped on Holyfield's right ear and spit a rather large piece onto the canvas or into the stands. I couldn't tell which. Oh, did I mention? I was there!

One of my acquaintances was a high roller at Caesars, and he had two comped tickets. The seats were good, just a little elevated so we had a perfect sightline of the ring. I happen to love boxing, even though I was far from a pro when I boxed as a college kid.

While chaos ruled the ring after Tyson went after Holyfield's left ear, I knew what would happen next.

"Let's get out of here," I said to my friend.

"Why? What's happening is fun to watch. Tyson's going after all of the guards around Holyfield."

"I'm not talking about there, I'm talking about the fact that Tyson's fans are going to riot," I said. "It's going to get bad. I'm telling you."

He reluctantly agreed to leave the arena and head back to Caesars.

"This is really dumb," he said. "Nothing's going to happen."

He was wrong. Bad stuff happened.

We were just outside MGM when we heard what we thought were muffled gunshots. (I believe the police report said these noises were the sounds of champagne bottles being uncorked.) By the time we got back to Caesars, the corner where MGM Grand; New York, New York; Excalibur; and Tropicana sit was totally closed to traffic, both vehicular and pedestrian. A riot was happening inside the MGM Grand casino. Gaming tables were being overturned, chips were being stolen, more gunshots (or champagne pops) were going off, and innocent people trying to escape the madness were being pummeled. I wasn't inside, so I am not sure what actually happened—but the next day it was reported that a full-blown riot had ensued.

So who caused the riot? I have my ideas. I think they were Tyson's fans, disappointed in Tyson's disqualification for munching on Holyfield's ears, caught up in the overwhelming mob mentality and fully exhibiting the same anger and viciousness of their hero. I think these fans were the ones that went ballistic after the Tyson fight. I certainly don't think it was the high rollers with comped seats who were "popping champagne corks," turning over tables and stealing chips, or pounding helpless people to a pulp.

I'm happy I followed my instincts to get the hell out of there and go back to Caesars. Nothing good could have come from staying at MGM Grand while madmen took over the place until the cops could subdue them. I'll pop a couple of champagne corks to those cops for getting things under control.

Bullets Over Rio

Dominator and I had been playing an excellent double-deck game at the Rio, an extremely popular off-Strip casino. At one time the Rio was a locals' casino, much like Maxim, but the ownership had grander ideas. The hotel was an all-suite one (the first of its kind in Vegas), and two new buildings were constructed. The Rio started to advertise itself not as a locals' place but as a great—and sexy—resort destination. Casino players went for it, and the Rio became a happening place.

Over the years, the Rio had great blackjack games *and* crummy blackjack games—maybe management decided which games to offer based on the weather. I think it was the first casino that offered those testosterone-fueled young men a blackjack pit with scantily clad female dealers—so who cared if blackjacks only paid even money? Look at that pair!

During the particular trip in question, Dom and I teamed up against the Rio using a common bankroll. Each of us played two hands. We played for about two hours, probably about an hour too long, but luckily our action went unnoticed. We varied our bets quite a bit, but we never had the same amount on the table. Yes, violating my rule the two of us played at the same table. As I said, our betting styles were quite different, so it did not bring attention to us—or, more likely, no one in the pit really cared.

The session had gone up and down. By the time we left, we had won a small amount. As the beautiful AP always says, "Any win is a good win."

We walked around the front of the building to the side of the building where the valet cars are picked up. Before we turned the corner, we heard firecrackers going off. It was about 10:00 in the morning; who would be shooting off firecrackers at that ridiculous hour? More and more firecrackers went off, and then I noticed a gang of young men across the busy street exchanging gunfire with another gang of young men. It was not a philosophical debate but a scene out of *Scarface*.

"Holy shit," I said and turned to Dom. For some crazy reason Dom was walking toward the gun battle.

"What the hell are you doing?" I asked him.

"I want to see what's going on," he said.

"Get over here," I screamed. "Get over here. They're not so far away that those bullets can't just go over the street and hit you. Get over here behind this pillar. Don't be insane."

Dom realized that he had been nuts, trying to get a closer look at the battle. We stood behind the giant pillar outside of the Rio and just listened. I just hoped no bullets would ricochet across the street, hit the Rio, and then hit one of us. The gun battle lasted a long time, but then we heard the sirens of the police cars and the shooting stopped. We looked around the pillar.

"God, it looks like every cop in Vegas," Dom said.

"Let's get the car and get out of here," I said.

"Hey, man, we won some money," said Dom, slapping me on the back.

"And we're alive to spend it," I said.

"And we saw a great show," he said.

"Yeah, and a free one, too. I mean, Vegas has everything."

Cheating Dealers at the Golden Gate: A Moral Dilemma

I am going to let you decide the morality of what the beautiful AP and I did at the Golden Gate casino. I wish I knew the ethics of what I did, but you know what? I really am not sure of the morality. I keep going back and forth in my mind, to this day.

The Golden Gate is a small downtown Las Vegas casino, on the same side of Fremont Street as the upscale Golden Nugget. The Golden Gate is decidedly downscale. It's for the lowest of low rollers.

One summer they had a great single-deck game that the beautiful AP and I played. The Golden Gate did not have big players; indeed the highest-denomination chips in their chip racks were black ($100), and some even topped out at green chips ($25). If you are a relatively big player, you cannot play your normal amounts in a casino that looks at $100 as a significant bet.

But a good game is a good game, and we would stop by the Golden Gate between playing a session at the Horseshoe Casino, which was diagonally across the street from the Golden Gate, and the Main Street Station Casino, which was a couple blocks away. (Aside: Men, you must go to the bathroom at Main Street Station. The urinals are against a giant piece of the Berlin Wall. As you pee, you can savor capitalism's defeat of communism.) Both Horseshoe and Main Street Station also had great single-deck games during this time, so we had a one-two-three casino attack.

At Golden Gate I played two hands, and the beautiful AP counted, and my spread was $10 to $50 on each hand. We wouldn't spend more than a half hour there. Despite casinos often being card-counter crazy, the Golden Gate did not have an "eye in the sky" from which to watch players and dealers. I guess there were not enough blackjack tables to make that worthwhile. I think they had six tables, most of which were closed during the weekdays.

The young female dealer we had that particular day was pleasant. She thought of herself as a fast dealer but, as I wrote before, there is no such thing as a fast dealer. While she dealt, she was quiet but professional. We had been playing maybe 10 minutes when a dealer from the Horseshoe sat down at our table. We recognized him. I think we even played at his table. At that point our dealer became animated and happily engaged the beautiful AP and me in conversation.

As our dealer—let's call her Jane—dealt the cards, she just kept talking, about this, about that, about those other things. At first I thought she was practicing the art of being friendly. Maybe she was auditioning for a better dealer job at a higher-end casino. She seemed to delight in talking away as if it were a carefree day of picnicking. At first I thought, *Go figure.*

Single-deck games are dealt facedown, and when we looked at our hands, the Horseshoe dealer quickly turned his cards faceup and Jane scooped the cards up and paid him 3-to-2 on his black-jack. I thought she had made a mistake. I thought he had turned over two picture cards, not a blackjack, but maybe I was mistaken.

Two rounds later, Jane dealt out the cards, and the Horseshoe dealer flipped over his two cards—and I could see they were two picture cards—but Jane scooped up the cards and paid him 3-to-2 for his "blackjack." Jane continued to happily engage us in conversation. She had become quite a talker. I leaned over and kissed the beautiful AP's neck, whispering in her ear, "She's cheating with him, paying blackjacks on 20s."

Another round, and that time the Horseshoe dealer flipped over an 11 to double down against the dealer's up-card of 6. She hit him with a 6, scooped up his cards, and paid him as if his double-down had already won. Two rounds later Jane, still talking merrily away, rewarded another 20 with a 3-to-2 payout as if it had been a blackjack.

I stood up. "Oh, man, I have to stretch. I come to Vegas, and all I do is sit down at blackjack tables all day long."

"I'll stretch with you," said AP.

AP and I walked away from the table. Jane just kept dealing to the Horseshoe dealer.

"What should we do?" I asked AP.

"We should tell management," she said.

"What if management is in it with them?" I asked.

"What do you want to do?" she asked.

"I don't know," I said. "I don't know, let's just cash out and get the hell out of here."

I know how I handled that was morally ambiguous—or totally wrong...or totally right. I really don't know. I am guessing that I was morally wrong, but the "I don't want to get involved" reflex kicked in and I truly did not want to get involved in anything to do with dealers and cheating and casinos. I didn't want my name out there as someone who screwed a dealer who was trying to screw a casino. Vegas can be a small world sometimes—a very small world—just ask Paul Keen.

So we went back to the table and I took our chips. As I was picking up my chips, I turned to Jane and the Horseshoe dealer and said, "You two stay out of trouble." I nodded sagely and walked to the cage. I don't know if my farewell hit the mark because AP and I walked out of the casino onto Fremont Street.

"I have to pee," I said. "Let's go over to Main Street Station."

The Walter Thomason Camouflage

The late Walter Thomason was a maverick among blackjack writers. He believed firmly in his progressive betting methods, and his book *Twenty-First Century Blackjack* espouses progressive betting as the one way to beat the game of blackjack. Although progressive betting might be fun and might give you very big wins on certain nights, it does not change the game of blackjack to favor the player. However, don't tell Walter that. Some of the biggest brains in the blackjack world have gone head-to-head with Thomason, explaining why his concepts are wrong, but Walter would have none of it.

Walter was married to best-selling romance and mystery writer Cynthia Thomason, and they did book signings and talks titled "For Love or Money" where Cynthia talked about romance and Walter talked about romancing the casinos' money. Walter was an excellent speaker and was a guest speaker at several of my Frank Scoblete's Gamblers' Jamborees.

Walter and I played at Treasure Island quite a lot in the 1990s. The beautiful AP, Walter, and I had many great times, but I must say, as a card counter, my favorite time with Walter was playing in the high-roller room with him at one table and me at another. You see, Walter's progressive-betting method would often draw the suits from "upstairs" to see what he was doing. Walter loved this, as it gave him a chance to teach them his wonderful progressive-betting ways, which could not give him an edge but interested the casino bosses nevertheless.

Walter would expound on the theory behind his betting method and the bosses would nod knowingly whether they understood what he was saying or not. Walter would talk their ears off.

I have to say his greatest night and one of my most enjoyable nights came about three hours before he had to leave for his home in Florida. He was packed and ready to go, but he wanted to play another round before he left. He came down to the high-roller room with his carry-on luggage, plopped himself at a table directly across from where I was playing, and began his session.

And the gods came down from Mt. Olympus, because Mr. Thomason seemingly could not lose a hand. I believe he started with a single $100 bet, and slowly that bet increased and increased; then it went to two bets that increased and increased; and then it went to three bets that increased and increased. At some point in time, he was playing every spot at the table with rapidly increasing bets on most hands. Yes, he did lose some hands, but overall not only did he win consistently, but every casino executive came down to watch. It was the Super Bowl of progressive betting.

Walter loved every minute of it. He lectured them on what he was doing; he explained in great detail the intricacies of why he bet this amount or that amount on this or that hand and when he would spread out his bets to cover other spots. There were even other players who paused in their games to watch Walter's amazing streak.

And what was I doing at the time at the table right across from his? I was all alone, just the dealer and me, playing an extremely aggressive game because no one bothered to look at my play. It was amazing. I am usually pretty cautious and I was certainly quite cautious at Treasure Island, but I took that opportunity to make money. I love playing when no one watches me. That's the purest blackjack game in the world. That's like playing on your dining room table.

I was not winning anywhere near what Walter won, but I had a great night. When some of the bosses ambled over to my table, I colored up and went over to join the crowd that watched Thomason. His streak continued.

"I got to get going," he would say and then keep playing.

"I got to get going," he would say again and then keep playing.

"I got to get going," he would say and then continue playing.

"Hey, Walter," I said. "You got to get going. You're going to miss your plane."

Reluctantly, Walter colored up and carried his truckload of chips to the cage, cashed out, and took the limo to the airport. I always enjoyed getting together with him. He had a sparkling personality, and he was the second-best cover for my advantage blackjack play—just a step or two behind those celebrities.

Walter Thomason was an original. There was no one like him.

I Am One Sexy Dude

We liked to play at the Riviera one summer, but the one time we stayed at the hotel we were not pleased. The hallways were dark—kind of like the hallways in the movie *Barton Fink*. But a good game is a good game. You don't ever pass those up if you can help it.

One late afternoon we were playing an excellent double-deck game when a woman, revealingly dressed—actually her ample, somewhat wrinkled huge breasts were almost popping out of her blouse—sat down at the table. She cashed in—leaning over the table to give the male dealer a close look at her mammary glands.

The beautiful AP and I smiled at her, as we would smile at anyone who sat down at our table. She winked at me. I don't know how old she was, maybe in her late forties, but she acted like a sex kitten.

"You have a handsome boyfriend. Husband?" she asked.

I held up my left hand to show my wedding ring.

"I'll bet he can make a woman happy," said the woman.

The beautiful AP just looked at her. That was a weird thing to say to someone's wife.

"My husband," the woman turned her head and looked over at the bar. "Oh, there he is." She pointed. Her husband, somewhat chubby, with male-pattern baldness, wore an open Hawaiian shirt with a big chain and medal dangling in the hairs of his chest. "Big boy!" she called. He looked over and shrugged his shoulders.

I noticed there were a lot sleazy and provocatively dressed people at the bar.

"Making reservations!" he called.

The woman fluttered her eyelids and said, "Oh, he is so funny."

"Where are you going to dinner?" I asked.

"Anywhere I have something good to eat," she nodded and winked.

"Are you here on a vacation?" AP asked. It's always good to carry on conversations as you count cards because many casino folks don't realize that this can be done. It's like riding a bike and talking to the person riding next to you. Yes, you can ride and talk at the same time.

"The convention, honey," she winked. "Aren't you two with the convention?"

"What convention?" I asked.

"There's a convention here?" asked the beautiful AP.

"You know, *the* convention."

"What convention?" I asked.

"Oh, never mind," she said. She took her chips and left the table.

I asked the dealer, "What convention is she with?"

"You're kidding, right?" he asked.

"No," I said.

"It's a swingers convention; you know, where couples exchange partners or have orgies...that kind of convention."

The beautiful AP and I turned around simultaneously. There they all were throughout the casino—talking, laughing, looking around for their game.

"I thought the people looked different," I said.

"You can see what they look like," said AP, shaking her head. "This is sad."

"To each his own," said the dealer.

"Hey, you got me, kid," I said to the beautiful AP, using my Humphrey Bogart imitation.

"Oh, Mr. Scobe, you are one sexy dude," said the beautiful AP, and she winked.

Exploit the Craziness

Casinos attract some seriously nutty people—folks who can't control their tempers, men or women who think the fates are out to get them, individuals who just don't have a clue about how to comport themselves in public. Bad manners, silly behavior, and stupid ideas can be tolerated in children—children younger than three—but when you have adults acting like two-year-olds, it is embarrassing. It is also a good moment if you can take advantage of such distractions.

One such crazy was a heart surgeon from California who threw a hissy fit—rather, he exploded like a nuclear weapon—when he had a cold streak one afternoon at the Golden Nugget in Las Vegas. The man threw his drink at the dealer, though most of it landed on the table. (I hoped he wasn't that sloppy when he operated on people's hearts.) "You are fucking against me, you bitch! You cheating bitch!" the man yelled. The dealer blanched. She was shaken. She was dripping with whatever the guy had been drinking. The floor person came over with a towel to wipe up the spilled drink. The dealer took the towel and wiped off her face and then she started to wipe off the table.

The heart surgeon grabbed the towel and threw it at the dealer. She backed off, stepping further into the pit. The floor person was coo-cooing the heart surgeon, trying to get him to cool down: "There, there, sir, I know how you feel. Sometimes luck...just calm down, please. You're scaring people. Why not go to your room and take a nap? I can have security escort you. We'll cash your chips for you."

The guy did not cool down. The pit boss came over to talk to him. I couldn't catch what the pit boss said. The heart surgeon heard nothing either; instead he pushed the blackjack table as hard as he could, and it tilted on its edge, wavered, and turned over, spilling all the chips. He was screaming at the top of his lungs about how the casino cheated everyone and you had to be crazy to play there.

I was sitting two tables away from the heart surgeon. And what was I doing as all of this tumult happened? In positive counts, I was upping my bet in the single-deck game like a wild man. Even in small positive counts I went to my maximum bet. All eyes were on the nutty heart surgeon and his screaming and yelling. Dealers, floor people, and patrons stared. A small crowd had gathered far enough away from the ranting heart surgeon but close enough to him to enjoy the show.

"Keep dealing," I said to my dealer. "I don't want to listen to this. The guy is an idiot. He should be shown the door." (But not too soon!)

My dealer was in her forties, and I imagine she had seen most casino tantrums. She kept dealing and said, "He's a heart surgeon, supposed to be one of the best."

"I think he's inhaled too much anesthetic," I said.

"He's a big bettor and has lost a fortune here. If he were your average player, he would be thrown out or arrested."

In truth, I didn't care that he behaved like a raving idiot—for all I knew he might have been a raving idiot in real life as well. I did feel sorry for the dealer and the people who tried to calm him down. But the longer he put on his show, the more aggressive I could bet in positive counts. If someone caused a problem big enough to take the attention away from other tables, then it was my clear card-counting duty to take advantage of the situation.

Once at Silverton Casino, a woman at my table who had been drinking up a storm blabbered, blubbered, rolled her head, and passed out onto my lap and then slid to the floor, an inert mass. If you ever want to get sick and get immediate medical attention, get sick in a casino. The casinos usually have their own EMS crews. Within a half-minute a whole bunch of casino folks had come out to help the unconscious sot.

I simply said to the dealer, "Let's keep playing. I don't want to watch this," and I kept playing. In positive counts I doubled my normal highest bet because (again) all the bosses were busy with the drunk. By the time they loaded her onto the gurney, put an IV into her arm and oxygen over her nostrils, and she was whisked off to the hospital, I had played maybe a half-dozen decks. I am sure the emergency room diagnosed her with the "Las Vegas Flu," an illness that can be diagnosed by asking the following questions: "How long has the patient been awake? How much has the patient had to drink?" So many people get that illness in Vegas. It is not so good for them, but it certainly was good for me.

Fire Sale

In 1980 the MGM Grand Hotel (which became Bally's) had a devastating fire that killed 85 people. About three months later another fire broke out at the Las Vegas Hilton. This fire killed eight people and was caused by arson. (Maybe by the maniacal heart surgeon?) With these two deadly fires, Las Vegas made strong changes in its fire laws to protect people staying in hotels. They insisted that at the first sign of smoke, an alarm had to go off that would be heard all over the hotel and casino.

And that brings me to the fire at Maxim. Okay, there was no fire at Maxim that I know of, but one afternoon in the crowded casino, the fire alarm went off. It was more than a decade after the two worst fires in Vegas casino-hotel history. It was loud as all hell. I figured players would leap up and run for the doors. Not so. Players just stayed at their tables and machines. AP and I were just about to be dealt hands in a high count, and I didn't want the game stopped in that second. I'd risk it.

The beautiful AP stood up, looked around the casino, and asked the dealer why no one had gotten up.

"Nobody ever gets up," said the dealer. "Gambling is more important than their lives. Come on, you know that."

"Good, good," I said. "Let's play out this hand in case there really is a fire and we have to vacate the building." You always want to play hands in positive counts, fire or no fire. That's a rule I *always* live by.

Casino gamblers usually have to be prodded to leave casinos when the alarms go off. The dealers tend to just stay at their tables and continue dealing. Nothing seems to change except there is this incredibly loud siren going off, so loud it drowns out the slot machine noises. I have yet to see any casinos usher out their patrons. "Gambling is more important than their lives." True.

The Sad Old Party Girl

The beautiful AP and I were playing at the Sands Casino in Las Vegas before it was leveled to become the Venetian. Everyone knew the sands of time had run out for the Sands, and there were few players around.

Our dealer was an older woman with a sagging facelift. She had dyed blonde hair and wore her uniform in what might have been a sexy way had she retained any of her former sensuality. She had her buttons open about halfway down her blouse in order to show somewhat sagging but rather large breasts in a lacy bra. Her upper chest was wrinkled from too much sun and too much age.

I tried to picture her long before, in the Vegas of the past. What was she like? I guessed she was a doll—a sexy, tempestuous doll. I could see her dressed in those 1950s and 1960s clothes. I am sure she knew how to intrigue a man.

She flirted with me as she told us the story of her life. She had been what used to be called a "party girl," which meant the casino would set her up with high rollers, and what would be, would be—as they say. She was also "in the chorus" of several shows that she named.

"I knew Sinatra and Dean Martin and everyone. I partied with everyone, cutie," she said to me. "After a while I decided to become a dealer, and the casino was nice enough to hire me. I'm retiring when this place closes in a couple of weeks. That's the end of my dealing career. I was even in a couple of movies; you see me in the crowd scenes in the casino. I even got paid for that."

While she talked, she dealt deeply into the deck. Her hands were old person's hands—gnarly with stretched skin, liver spots, and noticeable bulging blue veins. She didn't seem interested in the game, and AP and I used a very aggressive bet spread. I don't think a floor person ever came over to our table during a round of play.

"You know, Sinatra and Dean Martin would be allowed to deal, and they always let the players win. The casino didn't care because the biggest players came when they were here. This joint was jumping!" she said, paraphrasing Fats Waller's song.

As AP and I played blackjack at her table, I felt sad for her. The Vegas she knew—of the Rat Pack; the great singers, dancers, and entertainers; and those fine gentlemen in tuxedos (even if some of the gentlemen were mobsters) and ladies in beautiful evening gowns—no longer existed. It had ended long before, and what was left of the Sands would be leveled to exist no more as well. The past easily gets buried in the sands of time.

The Best Player's Club Ever

Not everything AP and I did or saw had to do with blackjack. At the Rio in the early 1990s they did not have a player's club as casinos do now. Their slot and video poker machines were not wired up or linked to any central computer. Instead, you went to a cage, where you cashed in for coins and then went to play the machines. The Rio counted that as a buy-in, and when you came back and cashed out, they counted all the time you were away as your playing time.

Obviously, if you stayed away for a week, it would look suspicious, but an hour or two? Just great! It was best that you came back with losses (that made them feel better), even if those losses were actually sitting in your room for cashing in at some other time. Occasionally, you wanted to come back with a win. That made it look legitimate. To really make sure no casino suit figured you were screwing them, we sat at various machines and on occasion put in a few coins. The comps we received from doing this were amazing. We never paid for anything at Rio.

I don't know how many advantage players actually took advantage of that, but AP and I sure did. Sadly, this player's club was gone when we came back for our next visit, but while it was there, we enjoyed it—a lot!

The Bus and the Bias

The very day that the beautiful AP and I would find our first (and only) biased roulette wheel, we also saw the biggest, fattest, strangest thing at the Rio.

That morning we were leaving the hotel to drive to some casino to play blackjack. We passed the only open roulette wheel, and I noticed on the scoreboard that three numbers had come up two or three times each. I laughed and said to AP, "Look, a biased wheel!"

To leave by the Rio's side entrance, we had to pass the gloriously inexpensive, absolutely delicious Rio buffet, which by that time had garnered great praise all over Las Vegas. We went out the door but couldn't get across the street because a bus pulled up in front of us. The bus looked really off-kilter, as it noticeably leaned toward the curb. When the doors opened, the fattest people I have ever seen in my life came trundling down the steps.

Look, I am somewhat overweight, but I would appear anorexic compared to those who stepped off the bus and onto the sidewalk. That bus looked as if it could tip over as massive one after massive one made their exits.

I could overhear some of them talking. They were going to the buffet for breakfast. Certainly not stupid on their parts. For $3.95 they could enjoy an all-you-can-eat buffet of the highest gastronomic variety. If eating's your thing, then this place would be your thing, too. Naturally, it was their thing.

So AP and I played our morning session and we came back to the Rio, figuring we'd have lunch, then go up to our room to take a nap. It was lunchtime, and the cost of the buffet was somewhat higher.

We entered the buffet, and there they were: the same boatload of biggies stuffing gigantic portions of lunch down their throats! I turned to the waiter and asked him, "The, uh, large people that are over there," I nodded my head in their direction. "Have they come back here for lunch?"

He shook his head and said, "No, they've been here for the whole time. First breakfast, now lunch."

"Do you think they'll stay for dinner?" asked AP, a half-joking tone in her voice.

"Oh, yeah, they always stay for dinner," he said.

After our lunch we passed the roulette tables again, and there were two open. I checked the scoreboards, and amazingly the three numbers I had seen were still being hit a few times on the original table. I said to AP, "Those are the numbers from this morning, right?"

"Yes," she said.

So we went up to our rooms and took a nap. When we came down to go for our afternoon session, those numbers were showing on the scoreboard. I looked at AP. She looked at me. I nodded. She nodded. We sat down, bought in, and started to place those three numbers.

Immediately one of them hit, which is a 35-to-1 payout. About five spins later another of the numbers hit; another 35-to-1 payout. It took off from there! We just kept playing those numbers, and we slowly started to increase our bets.

Streaks happen in all of gambling, so at first the pit didn't seem all that interested. I am guessing that particular table had not been played by anyone who took advantage of those same numbers coming up so frequently throughout the day. While AP and I played, there were several other players, and despite the fact that our numbers (I had started to consider them *our* numbers) were hitting, the other players just kept playing whatever system they played. Most of them were losing, too. The beautiful AP and I were winning; then we were winning big and then bigger and then...

"I'm sorry," said the pit boss. "We're closing this table. We're opening another one over there. Sorry about that."

That was our first and only time on a biased wheel. The Rio had been a great place for us to stay and play and learn how to take advantage of everything we could take advantage of.

CHAPTER 12

Horrors!
The Bruising World
of Advantage Players

Advantage players are little Davids, and the casinos are these big monstrous Philistines—but little Davids can beat them with their slingshots if they can learn card counting, dice control, and other techniques. Certainly advantage players can't bring down the whole Philistine casino enterprise, but they can win some money.

Sometimes I like to think of the casinos as dragons with shining gold teeth, and the advantage player's job is to extract as many of those teeth as he can.

Of course, the casinos will hate you if they learn you can beat them. You understand that, right? Advantage players are the scum of the earth to the casino bosses. Card counters are evil in their minds. That comes as no surprise to most good casino players. Between movies and books, the savvy players—even if these players are not advantage players—are fully aware that those who can take it to the casinos to win money are often taken out of the casinos and told never to come back. Some are even told that if they do come back it will be considered trespassing and they will be arrested. That's the reality of the whole thing.

I've been there and done that. Sometimes they throw you out nicely, and sometimes it can get pretty damn scary. So let's take a little trip into the real world of the advantage blackjack players—meaning AP and me—taking on the real casinos who have real bosses running them. I don't care if these "bosses" are now corporate types because they often act like the organized crime folks of old. Maybe you won't get buried in the desert or thrown in the ocean or dumped in a cornfield or drowned in a swamp—then again, who knows?

About 10 years ago, a marketing executive at the Golden Nugget in Las Vegas was interested in bringing me in to do a Frank Scoblete Gamblers' Jamboree where great gambling writers would give classes and we'd have some small tournaments. Before we could seal the deal, I had to speak to the casino manager and clear it with him. Marketing is a different animal than the actual casino group. Marketing thinks globally; the casino guys think one table and one machine at a time.

The casino manager looked at me as if I had just eaten his children and said, "You have to be crazy. I don't want you here. You bring in the wrong kind of people. I don't want earners in here."

"Earners?" I had never heard that term before. "What are earners?"

"Card counters, the so-called dice controllers, that kind of player," he said.

"The Jamboree is not for them. It is a general fun weekend," I said. "We won't be doing much in the way of advantage play."

"But *they* will come—to meet you, if nothing else—and they will be in my casino," he said. "I don't even care if they are $5 players, you understand, I don't want anyone here who can beat us."

We never did hold the Jamboree at the Golden Nugget in Las Vegas. Interestingly enough, the Golden Nugget was the first casino I was ever banned from, the year before I played the great Maxim game.

The casinos hate smart. Smart is bad. Indeed, if casinos gave IQ tests at the door as players entered, they would celebrate all the ones who seemed to be dim-witted, as long as they had large enough checkbooks.

The stories of card counters being backroomed, beaten, harassed, and thrown out of their hotel rooms in the middle of the night are not fictions invented by the propeller hats looking for their version of military glory. In the past (mostly the past) awful things were done to law-abiding citizens by the casino executives and security forces obsessed with protecting their games from advantage players who were not doing anything illegal. Keep in mind: I am never advocating breaking the law. Card counting, dice control, and advantage Pai Gow poker and video poker strategies are not cheating methods. They are merely methods that take the casino games being offered and use ways to beat the casinos themselves—all legal ways.

The same smiling casino executive photographed with that smiling slot patron who has just won a million dollars on a machine will be the same guy snarling, foaming, sputtering, and spewing to a card counter whose expectation is $20 an hour, "We don't want you here, you are too good for us." This same executive will tell bigger players, "I'm reading you the trespass act, and if you show up here again, you will be arrested for trespassing." These are the same men and women who banned (or limited) Paul Keen's play for a few decades.

Playing in a casino is like being in high school again. The smart kids are hated, and the dumb ones rule the school—the *real* school, as in the hallways, lunchroom, gymnasiums, and most classrooms. Smart is bad. Dumb is good. The casinos are ploppy heaven. Think of the incredible competition in high school to be one of the stupidest kids but how few of the students had designs on being valedictorian. That same principle holds in the world of casino gambling. The principal of the casino longs for the dumbest players he can attract. Dumb players are actually not necessarily dumb people—just people who play games they can't beat, perhaps for more money than they should.

Card counters and other advantage players are the bane of the casinos' existence. Yes, the casinos offer games for the public to play, but when some members of the public figure out how to beat those games, the executives scream, "Get your fat [or skinny] butt out of our casino!" The casinos want losers. The casinos cater to losers. The casinos love losers. "You're a loser" is the biggest compliment a casino can give a player. "Now, here's a comp for you. Thanks for giving us your money."

Oh, yes, the casinos will boot policemen, firemen, teachers, doctors, nurses, military veterans, and Medal of Honor winners from their properties if these individuals can beat the games. Mother Theresa can count cards? Out! "Go take care of the poor people on the streets but don't dare come into our casino and beat us at blackjack."

The casinos will boot those who have fought in our recent wars, those who ran into the World Trade Center to save the lives of their fellow citizens from the monstrous terrorism perpetrated there. It doesn't matter who these citizens are, the response is the same: "Out! Out! Out! You are too good for our games!" The casino executives don't care that their fellow citizens are being singled out for using their brains to beat the casinos' games.

And to make matters still worse, our slimy politicians will go to Vegas and carouse with the casino bosses, the very same people who perpetrate the abuse that fellow citizens experience at their casino properties.

It's a disgrace.

It's un-American.

It's nauseating.

It's immoral.

It's also the truth.

Unfortunately, the law is on the casinos' side for the most part. These casino businesses are not public enterprises—they are private entities, and as such, they have the right to refuse service to anyone. They can't discriminate because of your race, gender, religion, or any sort of handicapping condition. But they can discriminate against your brain and your skill. Someone could be smart and in a wheelchair, and as long as the casino executive says, "You are too good for us" instead of "We don't want handicapped people here," he can roll that person right out of his casino.

The casino executives have several ways of handling a threat to their profits. They can "ask" you not to play blackjack, yes, but they also might say, "You can play any other game here," or, if they want, they can *tell* you to get lost and not come back to their property ever again. Casinos cannot, however, drag you into the backroom and pummel the living daylights out of you. In the past this happened to some unfortunate card counters, and even within the last dozen years or so, some advantage players have been dragged into backrooms and even been handcuffed to pipes. Remember this: If a casino stops you from playing and then "requests" that you come to the back room, you have the right to ask if they are calling the police. If they are, tell them you'll wait right where you are until the police arrive. Never go into a backroom or what is often called an "office." Stay on the casino floor.

Since card counting is not illegal, you cannot be arrested for such intelligent use of your brain. If a casino tells you to beat it, then just beat it. Don't argue with the executive tossing you—he isn't interested in your opinions. Don't even talk to the executive. And don't show him your Medal of Honor or plaque for saving the lives of your fellow Americans in the latest terrorist attack. It won't change his mind. You might be a hero to America, but to him you are a blackjack terrorist. Just take your chips and leave. You can come back the next day and cash in your chips. Or you can send a friend to cash in your chips. Leave.

Please keep this in mind: always be courteous. Never touch a casino employee in these situations, as the casino might press assault charges against you. Those massively rock-solid-muscled security people are very delicate, and the casino might accuse you of attacking them. Use your brain and just get out of the place.

Let me share with you some of the experiences the beautiful AP and I have had in the "we hate card counters" world of the casinos. These will help you see that being an advantage player is not all that glamorous or even enjoyable.

Even with our superb team play, AP and I did not escape the blackjack wars unscathed. We've been barred, we've been banned, we've been trespassed and abused. Advantage-play life can be rough. Our bannings go from relatively mild to outrageous to damn dangerous—and that's the order I put them in.

Our First Time: The Golden Nugget

Your first barring is like your first baby—something to treasure, a golden time period, a... Actually it isn't any of that. A first barring jangles the nerves; almost makes you feel a sense of shame, not that you were caught but that you dared to do this to the little, old people-loving casino. After all, the casinos exist to make you happy, and you just made them unhappy. That feeling doesn't last too long before the "Why offer a game and then not let me play it?" feelings come into play. Rarely does the "It's their place, so they can do what they want" idea come into play—at least at the start.

The beautiful AP and I were "wonging" games on the Las Vegas Strip one early afternoon. Wonging is a technique developed by Stanford Wong, where you don't play every hand but count the cards at one or two tables from behind the players. When the count becomes positive, you jump into the game with your bets. It's kind of like the "big player" technique without actually using a spotter or big player.

Both AP and I were able to count two tables each that were next to each other; thus we covered four in total. We'd count, jump in, and then get out if the count went negative. We'd only do this twice in each casino and then we'd head out the door.

We had great success at Flamingo Hilton (now called Flamingo Las Vegas). I jumped in the first time and I think I won almost every hand. AP jumped in the second time, and I think she won all of her hands. We each did this once more with similar results. Then we headed for the door.

"That was great," I said as I hugged the beautiful AP outside the Flamingo Hilton. "We kicked their ass!"

After a workout (sometimes we did our workouts after an early session of play) and a nap, we drove downtown to play at the Golden Nugget. We had been playing there every other day for a couple of weeks. There seemed to be no interest in our play, so we kept going back. They had great single- and double-deck games.

I loved playing there because one of the pit bosses (or floor man, I don't remember his title) was boxing referee Richard Steele. I had great conversations with him about all the matches he worked and the personalities of the fighters and famous managers. He was a hell of a nice man, and I had a lot of respect for him.

That particular afternoon the floor man, Michael Patti, opened a table just for us, saying, "We need to open another table, and you guys can play alone right now if you want to."

Being a complete and utter idiot, I went over to the other table with the beautiful AP. So we played. We were down $600 when Michael came up behind me and tapped my shoulder.

"Hey, Michael, I was going to ask you for a comp," I said.

He laughed and replied, "You can't play here anymore. I'm sorry, you guys are too good for us."

I pulled out the tried-and-true statement many card counters have used: "Michael, we're down $600."

He shook his head and said, "Doesn't matter. We can see what you can do."

"Crap," I said.

"Your first time?" he asked.

"Uh, ahm, uh," I mumbled.

"Yes," said AP.

"You shouldn't have jumped at having your own table. It made it too easy to observe your play. Also, you should be more aware of the fact that when you wong in certain casinos, they'll photograph you and send those pictures to other casinos. We have a great picture of you two from the Flamingo Hilton. We let you play just to make sure they had you right." He smiled and added, "They had you right."

"Crap," I said. I was really down—first for being caught and second for being caught because I was an idiot. Yes, I had read all about barrings and bannings, but I never really thought in my heart that it would happen to us. I thought we were so very clever. I was clever the way an idiot is clever. I should have known taking a table just for us was stupid. I should have realized that wonging up and down the Strip was stupid, too.

"You look depressed," Michael said.

"I am," I said.

"We both are," AP said.

"Okay, look," he said. "We took $600 from you. I'm going to give you a comp for $200 dollars to Stefano's, our Italian restaurant. That will cover a great meal and drinks. But stay away from Golden Nugget for as long as you're in town this trip. Okay?"

"Okay," said AP.

"I was a card counter," Michael said. "I know how you feel. But I still don't ever want to see you again."

This story does have an appendix that you might even call a somewhat happy ending. We had more than enough for dinner with that comp, so I ordered and drank most of two bottles of Pouilly Fuisse. I was high...no, I was drunk. As we came down the escalator, I needed to go to the bathroom and turned right. There was a bank of $1 machines called, interestingly enough, Treasure Island. I had some slot coins (I have no idea where I got those) and put three of them in. "Come on, come on," I said out loud as the reels spun.

The reels stopped. I looked through a drunken fog at the result. I won $1,600! I put all the coins in the bucket (in those days the machines actually used and paid in coins), cashed them in, ran to the bathroom, and barely made it. I could have put out a large fire.

Sadly, we never did play at the Golden Nugget again—at least, not blackjack. The Golden Nugget games started to deteriorate in the summers after this barring, so aside from walking through the place to keep cool, Michael Patti was the last person in the blackjack pit we ever talked to. Still, I did get to take home all that money from one lucky spin of a slot machine called Treasure Island. That must have been a foreshadowing of the casino where I would play for the longest time. That slot win more than made up for our loss at blackjack.

The Barbary Coast

I wasn't even playing high stakes when the following happened. The Barbary Coast, sitting right next to the Flamingo Hilton and on the corner of Las Vegas Blvd. and Flamingo Road, was a small casino featuring a great single-deck game. I woke up really early one morning and decided to walk over there and waste a little time. I figured I'd play for a half hour or so and then head back, wake up the beautiful AP, and we'd start our regular day.

I sat down at the only open table. There was one other man at the table, a Japanese fellow playing $1,500 per hand. He had a translator with him; he must have been some kind of big shot. The Barbary Coast was not exactly the type of casino where a player bet that much, but I guess the casino knew it had a nice fat fish on the line, so why not let him play?

I bought in for $300 and put out a $5 bet. I figured I'd go from $5 to $25 on my spread. No casino would bother with someone betting that low, especially when that someone was sitting next to a guy who was probably dropping tens of thousands of dollars. I even figured in really high counts I might go to two hands of $25. I thought I would have no trouble getting away with my daring ploy. In casinos used to small action, you had to give them small action—that's a rule one should follow. (Yes, another rule I occasionally break.)

The very first time the count got high was in the second round of play. I went from $5 to $15, the bet my count called for. I won that hand. The count stayed high, and I put out another $15 bet. The floor person walked over and pushed my bet back to me. I pushed the bet back to my betting circle. He pushed the bet back to me. I looked at him. He looked at me and said, "We don't want your action here."

I took my chips, cashed them, and left. A single increase in a bet, and I was walking down the Strip wondering what went wrong. I chalked it up to the Barbary Coast being paranoid—I guess justifiably paranoid. I also hoped that Japanese big shot got on a lucky streak and creamed that rotten place.

"We're Counting Cards, We're Counting Cards"

Dustin Hoffman's Raymond Babbitt in *Rain Man* said it better than I can: "We're counting cards, we're counting cards." I think I met my own Rain Man. I am guessing the kid had Asperger's syndrome, a form of autism characterized by a lack of social graces. Some Asperger's sufferers seem noticeably different—not dangerous, but off, not there, maybe out of it. People with Asperger's can make things uncomfortable for those around them without knowing they are doing so.

Anyway I am guessing the person at the blackjack table with us had Asperger's because he did everything a card counter shouldn't do, and he did it loudly. He was either nuts or he had Asperger's.

I was at the Mirage one early evening. The table was almost full: a grandmotherly woman in a blue dress, a polo-shirted man in white shorts, me (playing two hands), and a young man of about 25 dressed in camouflage.

When the young man came to the table, he announced, "I am very good at this game. Follow me. I am very good at this game." I certainly heard a small hint of Rain Man in his voice. He looked a little feverish, too, but I tossed that up to the 107-degree temperature outside. Since I know several people with Asperger's Syndrome, I figured he had it, judging by his somewhat distracted look and the sound of his voice.

The dealer dealt the cards. Since a single-deck game is dealt facedown, I had no idea what cards the other players had. However, once everyone was finished playing their hands, the dealer went around the table, turned over everyone's cards, and paid those who had won—in this case all of us because the dealer busted.

After looking at the cards I knew the count was a +3. I put out $200 on each of my hands.

"The count's a +3, a +3," Rain Man said. "Everybody, the count is a +3."

Oh, shit, the guy had the count right.

"Put up a big bet. The count is a +3."

The other two ignored him, and I quickly took my bets to $50 each. I didn't want to get nailed because our Rain Man had announced what the count was. He had put up a $30 bet since his low bet was $10.

As fate would have it, he got a blackjack; I busted on both of my hands, and I really don't remember what the other two got.

The dealer shuffled the deck.

"Everybody, follow me," said Rain Man. "Follow me when I bet. I know what I'm doing. We'll make some money here."

The count went low right away, and I kept up my smallest bet.

"The count is negative," said Rain Man. "I don't bet in negative counts. Nobody should bet."

Everybody bet except him. The dealer looked at him for a prolonged moment. He certainly could tell the kid was off, but I didn't know if the dealer counted cards while he dealt and therefore realized that our very own Rain Man was correct on the count. Very few dealers know how to count (some don't even know the correct basic strategies) and very few of those few who do count bother to do it. Why waste the energy?

The third round of play saw another high count.

"High count. Positive count," called out Rain Man.

The floor person came over. The dealer whispered something in his ear.

"Raise your bets," said Rain Man. "Positive count." He again went to $30 on his bet.

"Should I raise my bet?" the grandmotherly woman asked the dealer.

The dealer shrugged and replied, "It's your money."

She doubled her bet to $100. That round saw her get a blackjack, and she clapped her hands. "You know what you're doing," she said to Rain Man.

Rain Man lost his bet. I lost mine, but I didn't raise my bet. I began toying with the idea of leaving the table after a couple more rounds if Rain Man stayed. It is verboten to even mention card counting at a blackjack table; it is a mortal sin to actually announce that you are doing it, tantamount to talking about bombs when you're at the airport or in a plane.

The next time the count zoomed up, Rain Man stood up and put down a $50 bet. He said, "This is it. Big count! Big count!"

The grandmotherly woman went to $200. "You should bet big, you should bet big," he said to me and the man in the white shorts. I shrugged my shoulders and said, "Okay, okay." I put out $100 on each hand. I shook my head at the dealer to make it appear that I was just placating an idiot. I wish I'd had the guts to put up two hands of $300 because the count was through the roof. The man in the white shorts ignored Rain Man. He just kept betting his flat $100. I figured that would be my last round. The floor person was standing there, and then another suit came over and watched the game. I figured he was the pit boss. I just kept shaking my head to make it look like I had no idea what the kid was doing.

I got a blackjack, and so did Rain Man. I think the dealer had a 16 and busted. Everyone won. "See, see," said Rain Man. "High count means you can win a lot."

Before the dealer could deal the next round, the pit boss came around the table and touched Rain Man on the shoulder. Rain Man almost jumped through the roof and said, "You scared me, you scared me."

"Sir, can you step away from the table, please?" said the pit boss in a low voice.

"I want to play blackjack," said Rain Man. "I've been studying it and I want to play blackjack."

"Step away from the table, please," said the pit boss, with a little more authority in his voice.

The dealer just stood there looking straight ahead, a wooden statue. The man in the white shorts got up and went to another table; so did the grandmotherly woman. As she picked up her chips, she said, "You should stop mistreating that poor young man. You can see there is something wrong with him." The dealer ignored her and looked straight ahead.

I sat and watched. Would Rain Man leave, would he be "escorted" out, or would the police be called? I didn't think Rain Man had any idea of what was happening. Then a woman came over.

"What's happening?" she asked. "I'm his mother."

The pit boss paused. The floor person watched, and even the dealer turned his head to see what was about to transpire.

"Ma'am, your son is too smart for the game of blackjack. He can play any other game in the casino but not blackjack," the pit boss said.

She nodded and said, "That's the first time he's ever been too smart for something." The pit boss actually seemed embarrassed, one of the few times I ever saw a pit boss look embarrassed.

"Terry," the woman said to her son, "we have to go now."

"I want to play blackjack," Terry said.

"We have to go now, Terry. Come on." She took his chips from the layout and put them in her purse. "Come on, Terry, we have to go now."

"Color me up," I said.

The following week I got the boot from Mirage. It happened in the blink, maybe two blinks, of the eye. I was playing at a $25 two-deck game not far from the craps tables. I had two hands of $25, and I intended to go to $200 on each but in gradual steps, not hopping, skipping, or jumping them. The Mirage had a great game but a bad reputation.

I played through several shuffles—only once did the count get high enough for me to double my bet. That was it. Finally after the fourth shuffle, the count started to go up. I went to $50 on each hand, won those, and then went to $100. I won one, lost one. I put out $125 on each hand. Two real hands came across the table and pushed back my bets. I looked up. It was the same pit boss who had bounced Terry the week before.

"Can I speak to you, sir?" he asked, and pointed to the area behind the other players. I got up. I knew what was coming.

"Sir, you're too good for us. You can't play blackjack here anymore. You're free to play any of the other games."

I nodded, colored up my chips, and left.

The Sands in Atlantic City

The casinos in Atlantic City can't bar you, they can't ban you, they can only screw you—that is, they can make the game impossible to beat by changing certain rules. Once Ken Uston won his battle against the casinos in 1979, it looked as if Atlantic City would become a mecca for card counters. It became anything but; in fact, it became the butt of jokes from counters who plied the Vegas casinos: "You play Atlantic City? You poor man. Do they have any beatable games?"

Over the years, Atlantic City brought in eight-deck games, which are monstrosities. Certainly they can be beaten, but it takes the patience of Job (who ultimately lost his patience in the story) and a bet spread that is a monstrosity as well. Even such games require decent penetration. If they cut three of the eight decks out of play, you're whistling Dixie.

Still, Atlantic City card counters who could afford it played the high-roller rooms' six-deck games, which were far better than the eight-deckers on the main floor. They also tended to have slightly better rules for splitting pairs.

But times kept changing. Atlantic City still can't bar or ban counters, but they can legally do the following:

- Have the floor person talk to you to distract you. This might distract some counters. I never found talking and counting to be a problem.

- Bring in a fast dealer to make it impossible to follow the cards. I've said this already: there is no such thing as a fast dealer if you just keep your eyes on the cards. If you watch the dealer, she can appear fast but that is just her body moving. Cards stay on the table a long time no matter how fast the dealer seems to be. Even when a person busts and the dealer scoops up the lost hand with a flourish—it's still slow-motion.

- Shuffle up after every hand. This eliminates any card counter's ability to win. Of course, it also screws up the casino's ability to make money if other players are at the table—one hand, then a six-deck shuffle, then one hand, then a six-deck shuffle. Some card counters, out of pique, will get up and go to another table, where the dealer is then informed to do the same thing. I never did that. If they shuffled after every hand, I stopped playing. There is no point in being obnoxious to the casino personnel who are just "following orders."

- Tell you that your bet can't go higher than table minimum. If you are at a $100 table, you can only bet $100—but other players at that table can bet all the way up to table maximum.

At the Sands in Atlantic City, I got just about all of the above tactics used against me one afternoon. That Sands, just like the Sands in Las Vegas, is no more. The Vegas one became the Venetian; the Atlantic City one became a vacant lot. The last days of the Atlantic City Sands were sad. The main floor didn't even have carpeting that matched. The place looked dirty, and the employees looked as if they had been transformed into zombies.

I was playing a six-deck game with decent penetration. I spread my bets from one to 12, again not in big jumps. A floor woman came over and struck up a conversation with me. Since I was not alone at the table, everyone got into it. I actually don't remember what we discussed.

That didn't work. Then they brought in "Speedo" a dealer who was thought to be fast, but it had no effect on me. (I should have seen what was happening, but I didn't. Sometimes I can't believe how stupid I can be.)

Then another suit came over. "You can't bet more than table minimum," he said. Then he turned to the dealer and said, "Shuffle," which meant to shuffle after every hand. I looked at the guy and shook my head. Sands was a dump; it was about to close. This guy would probably lose his job. I shook my head again and colored up. "I have to protect the game," he said. "You understand, I have to protect the game."

The beautiful AP and I did have another interesting experience at the Sands one winter. There had been a big snowfall, and during the day some of the snow would melt because of the sun and then freeze into solid patches of ice at night.

We had some complimentary stay in a suite at the top of the hotel. By that time the Sands had gone severely downhill, but a free suite is a free suite. We did not intend to play any of the Sands' games, but again, a free suite is a free suite.

In the middle of the night, the fire alarm went off—a piercing sound. Both AP and I jumped up. "We have to get out of here," she said.

We were both in our pajamas and we opened our door slowly to check for any smoke in the hallway. We were okay. We ran to the exit stairs and made our way down lord knows how many stairs. At the bottom of the stairs we pushed the emergency door, which opened onto an alleyway covered in ice!

"Yeeeeooooooohhhhh!" we screamed as both of us slipped onto our butts and headed down the slanted alleyway toward the street. While it was the "middle of the night" for us, it was still prime time for casino players, many of whom were waiting for cabs or their limos to take them wherever.

As we came hurtling out of the alleyway, we became the center of attention—two maniacs in pajamas sliding on their butts into the street. When we stopped, we stood up with dignity, though both of our asses were soaking wet from the ice. We then walked into the Sands' lobby with our heads held high and our hands trying to cover up our wet butts.

In the elevator an older woman asked us, "What were you doing?"

"The alarm went off," AP said.

"The alarm," I said.

"No one listens to the alarms," she said.

The AC Hilton: No More Comps for You

While I often did not stay at the hotels where I played and I also did not hand in players cards at casinos where I did play, these were rules of mine that I frequently violated. (I don't know why I make rules and then violate them. It must have to do with not wanting to follow authority even if I *am* the authority.)

I loved playing at the Atlantic City Hilton. The casino had excellent six-deck games with amazingly deep penetration in the high-roller room. I had RFB, which meant I was a big shot—and, of course, a fool to think I could go back to the same casino time and time again and have no one notice what I was doing.

The last time I played there, no one said I could only flat-bet, no one told the dealer to shuffle up, and no fast dealer was brought in. But the next time I called my host, he told me that the Hilton would no longer comp me rooms or food or anything, for that matter. "Frank," he said, "I'm sorry, but they don't want you here. We can't stop you from coming, but they don't want you here."

That was that. I figured the next time I showed up I'd get the fast dealer, one-bet rule, and a shuffle after every hand. So there was no point in showing up at the Hilton again.

Foxwoods and the Power of Television

I was becoming well known. I had quite a few books out that were strong sellers. I had been on television quite a few times and was doing a weekly radio show.

Someone from Turner Broadcasting called me and wanted to know if I would be interested in doing a television segment about blackjack for CNN and TBS to be filmed at Foxwoods Casino in Connecticut. I immediately said yes. I had never been to Foxwoods, so it would give me a great reason to go, and obviously a television interview for TBS and CNN would help the sale of my books. All writers know this: publicity = book sales.

The Turner Broadcasting lady who met me at Foxwoods seemed upset. "Is everything okay?" I asked.

"We're having a problem," she said.

"What is it?"

"They don't want you here," she said. (I know, I know, sounds just like the Atlantic City Hilton.)

"What do you mean?"

"The executive who's in charge of this said, 'We don't want Scoblete. He can't come on our property.'"

"I've never played here before," I said.

"He just kept repeating that they don't want you here: 'We don't want Scoblete.'"

"But here I am," I said.

"We had a deal with them to film in the casino, and they were ready to renege on it if we brought you in."

"Amazing," I said. "So what is it? I'm out?"

"We had long meetings and discussions with them. Here's what we did, if you'll agree to it. We can film our segments here, but you must have two security guards with you at all times. You will not be allowed to play any of the games. In exchange for your coopera-tion, you can stay the night, do the filming, stay the second night, but then you must go. When you eat, they will stand outside the restaurant and make sure you don't leave on your own."

I laughed. "I hope these guys won't be in the hotel room with me."

"They will be outside the door."

Two security guards assigned to me for two straight days—amazing! I didn't realize I was that important a person.

As we entered the hotel, sure enough, there they were—my first two security guards. They would rotate with a third guard so they could take breaks, but two would always be glued to my side. Obviously there was more than just one unit. I am guessing three to cover 24 hours of watching the supremely dangerous me and protecting Foxwoods, which at that time, I believe, was the biggest casino in the world.

The next day, we filmed. I went to a blackjack table with my two security guards attached to my hips. The director of the film-ing said, "You two guys, can you move away from him? You're in the shot."

The guards moved an inch or so.

The director shook his head. "He can't do anything. He's just going to discuss how to play blackjack and the best strategies. It's no big deal." He moved his arms outward. "If you could just step over some more so you aren't in the shot."

The guards moved another inch or so.

We filmed. Those of you who have made movies or done television know that filming even a short segment takes time. You go over and over the same stuff because the lighting wasn't perfect or the angle of the camera wasn't perfect or you weren't perfect. Those two-hour movies you see usually take several months to make—some take substantially longer.

When the segment appeared on television, sure enough—one of the security guards was in the shot. As far as I know, the segment appeared once and was never used again. That symbolically represented my experience at Foxwoods. I appeared for two days and then never went back again.

Tunica: The Fitzgerald's Trespassing

Long ago in a casino town far, far away, Tunica was the best venue to play blackjack and craps in the country. I loved the Horseshoe, the Grand, and Sam's Town; actually I loved just about all of the Tunica casinos.

Fitzgerald's had the second-biggest property of all the hotel-casinos behind only the mighty Grand. The casino was not very large, but it tended to be crowded all the time. I think they had a cheap buffet, which players flocked to, but the casino itself didn't really appeal to me. It seemed kind of dingy. Or maybe that is just a particularly bad experience clouding my general memory of the place. You decide.

The Dominator and I were playing blackjack in the high-roller room. Dom was wearing one of his patented disguises. He looked like a really dopey, nerdy type of guy, complete with a penholder in his top pocket. In fact, I put just a smudge of ink on his shirt to make it look even more realistic. He wore thick-framed Barry Goldwater glasses.

Two days before the incident I'll recount here, we had been told at the craps table that we were not allowed to shoot the dice anymore. We could bet on other shooters, but our shooting days at

Fitzgerald's were over. Dom got annoyed; Dom gets annoyed very easily. He fumed, "You mean to tell me you want us to bet our money at craps but not shoot the dice? Shooting is the most fun."

Dom had not yet—if he ever will—learned the primary lesson: when the casino says you can or can't do something, well, then you can or can't do that something. Casino floor people, pit people, shift managers, and casino managers can tell anyone that they can't shoot the dice or play craps at their casino, or they can tell you to get lost and never come back. Dom just couldn't sit well with that power structure. Dom has serious problems with authority.

This incident came during the "Week of the Great Mississippi Banning" when Dom and I were banned from all the casinos in Tunica and told by a casino suit at Gold Strike that our banning would be for all the casinos in Mississippi. The bannings came mostly at craps tables, but one occurred at Pai Gow poker (Sam's Town), and the Fitzgerald's boot came at the blackjack table.

Fitzgerald's was the first of the bannings, and so we did not see it as anything other than a *Well, we won't be playing that place ever again.* We didn't realize it would herald our good-bye to Tunica and that our Deep South banning tour was about to begin.

In addition to Dom and me at the table was an exceedingly nice, chatty woman of about 70 years old. She evidently had some money because she was betting $100 per hand. The table was a $25 minimum, and Dom and I each played two hands. He played each hand for $25 a hand, and I played each for $50 a hand. Our spreads would be eccentric; we moved our bets differently, and we had no trouble playing at the same tables in Vegas or Tunica. At Fitzgerald's we pretended not to know each other.

At that point in time, we were both using the wonderful Speed Count. It was a somewhat protective method, though not as strong as Hi-Lo in making money. Speed Count, unfortunately, did not protect us at Fitzgerald's.

We had probably played through two shuffles when a sour-faced woman showed up at the table. There was nothing subtle about her approach. She did not ask us to leave the table so she could talk to us to tell us we were not welcome to play in her casino. Instead, she yelled at Dom, "You don't think I know who you are? You don't fool me. I know who you are!"

"What?" asked Dom, feigning ignorance. His acting skills would not be effective with her. She had nailed him. I ignored her harangue and put out my bet. After all, I wasn't with the ink-stained-pocket, thick-glasses Barry Goldwater man. She pushed my bets back. "Everyone knows who *you* are!" she screamed at me.

I took my chips. We'd been made.

"I don't know what you're talking about," said Dom.

"You two are together. Frank and Dom, we know who you are. I am now going to tell you that you will be considered trespassing the very next time you set foot on Fitzgerald's property. That is anywhere on our property."

Dom scooped up his chips.

"Let me color you up," said the dealer. Dom just sneered at her. I put my chips back on the table and let her color me up.

The sour-faced executive then went into the trespassing thing again. The woman at the table said, "What are you doing? These men are very nice. They weren't cheating. Why are you treating them this way?"

"This is none of your business," she said to the woman.

"I would just like to know what's going on," said the woman.

"This is none of your business."

"You just do this to players who have done nothing wrong?"

"This is none of your business."

Dominator, never short of blasting dragon breath at dragon-like people, said to the nice woman, "We can beat their fucking game, and she doesn't want us to play. They did it at craps, and now they're doing it at blackjack. We can't come back here." He snarled at the supervisor, "This place is a fucking shit house anyway." Dom is not subtle.

Four security guards came over. Dom had his chips in his hand and a security guard on each side of him. They were big guys. They walked him to the cage to cash out. I had two security guards on each side of me, though one seemed so old I thought he would die before we got to the cage. None of the guards said anything to us.

Once we had cashed out, my old withered security guard said, "We'll walk you down the road to the gate and see you leave the property. You are never to come back."

I held up my hand. "We have a friend here. He can drive us." That was best-selling author Henry Tamburin. I wasn't going to his table (that might get him booted), so when we exited the building, Dom gave Henry a call on his cell phone. The old security guard said, "Normally we would walk you out, but your friend can pick you up down there near the gate."

And so our trespassing at Fitzgerald's started us on the road to ruin in Tunica, Mississippi. Thankfully Henry Tamburin was there to drive us off into the sunset—actually moonlight, as it was nighttime.

Circus Circus, and I'm the Clown

On the Las Vegas Strip, I was playing at the sleazy, berserk-child-infested Circus Circus casino, which was offering an excellent single-deck blackjack game. I had heard that the place was going to change the game in a few days to a six-deck game of a much poorer quality. I had never played the place before, but I figured why not take my shot at their good game before it disappeared. The beautiful AP, who had standards, said, "I'm sorry, but there are a lot of great games in Vegas. I'm not playing in that dump. The adults are overtired, and the children are berserk."

Circus Circus was a bad idea whose time should never have come. It was a resort geared toward children. Parents who could not restrain their gambling habits would bring their little ones to the place, where they would run wild. Maybe when Circus Circus was first built it was supposed to appeal to adults, having circus acts leaping, riding, and swinging over your heads when you played. But that evidently did not work out well, and a ceiling was placed above the players' heads. Leaping, riding, swinging circus acts were distracting and somewhat scary, as the performers might land on gamblers' heads should they fall.

So I went to Circus Circus alone. The beautiful AP was right— overtired adults and wild-eyed children. But the Circus Circus blackjack game was good. I decided to let it all hang out and go for the big score in a fast and furious way. I mean I was going to go wilder than the kids I saw running about and screaming.

I started playing two hands at $5 each. With the first positive increase in the count, I went up in huge leaps. So when the true count was +1 (or any initial plus count), I went to $50 on both hands; when it was +2, I went to $100 on both hands; and when it was +3, I went to $200. I maxed out at two hands of $300. I figured I'd burn out my welcome quickly, as the place was known for its paranoid pit people and executives. Counters and winning non-counters were shown the door so often the normal door looked as if it were revolving.

As fate would have it, those increases in my bets won right away. I went on a torrid winning streak. I got to play three games before I saw a parade of suits heading for the table. I knew I was about to be booted, so I threw a tip to the dealer, scooped up all my chips, and headed for the cage.

One casino suit with a Groucho Marx mustache that made him look ridiculous instead of alluring or witty followed me right to the cage and stood behind me. Even without looking behind me I could feel the guy's glare on my neck. As I cashed my chips, he moved to my right, and I could see him counting them. He almost growled at me and was about to speak. I ignored him. I turned, putting my extremely thick wad of $100 bills into my pockets and headed out the side door. I'll admit it—I did have a slight smile on my face, which old Groucho saw. How could I not? It was a nice score done unsubtly by a player who knew he never would go back to that casino.

Next door to Circus Circus were a couple of little casinos, Slots A Fun and Westward Ho. I went in the side door of Slots A Fun, and damn if Groucho didn't follow me—he was maybe 25 feet behind me. He had an intense look on his beady-eyed face. I left that little casino out the front door and started going south on the Strip. He continued to follow me. I passed the Westward Ho. He was still following me. What was the matter with this guy? I won the money fair and square—it wasn't even his money.

This happened in the early 1990s, and I was not slightly overweight as I am now. (Okay, okay, I am now more than slightly overweight.) At the time, I was still hitting the heavy bag, though my boxing career had long ended (in my brutal beating, I might add). I ran five- to 10-mile races. I was in great shape, and I knew I could beat up the creep. I became a little annoyed, bordering on angry, so I turned and walked right at him. I looked him in his weasel-red eyes and finally said, "What are you going to do? Huh? What are you going to do?" He spun around and headed back to his casino. Of course, had this happened yesterday as opposed to back then, I would have to say, "Go away, please, or I will belly-whomp you...with your permission, of course. Unless you'd like to join me at the buffet, my treat?"

He was probably tailing me to get the license plate of my car and maybe find out my name. Anyway, that is what I am guessing. I had done nothing wrong. It is not against the law to be a good player, but tell that to the industry that creates the games that can be beaten and then gets angry that some players have the nerve to then beat those games.

Life is unfair. But in the next incident, life—blackjack life—can also be terrifying.

The Horseshoe in Las Vegas

In the early 1990s the beautiful AP and I were playing in a downtown Las Vegas casino that prided itself on taking any kind of action any kind of player wished to play. It was the "unafraid" casino. That's right: the Horseshoe. You could supposedly walk in and make a million-dollar bet, and no one would blink. Indeed, some great stories have been told over the decades about such casino fearlessness in the face of big gamblers. The casino owner publicly prided himself on his fearlessness in accepting all kinds of bets from all kinds of players.

His casino offered a great one-deck blackjack game, and the beautiful AP and I played the place for a couple of weeks, doing different shifts so we wouldn't be noticed too much. Actually, we didn't worry all that much, because Horseshoe was supposed to be fearless in the face of players, right? I mean you publicize that you are fearless, so you should be fearless—I would think.

We were decent bettors by that time, going from $25 on one hand to two hands of $300 when the count called for it. We were typical card counters, of course, using the Hi-Lo card-counting system with some changes in playing strategies based on the count.

We were playing a single-deck game. I had two bets of $300 each on the layout. Suddenly the dealer started throwing the cards into my face. He zipped the cards into my face fast as fast could be. Dealers dealing cards on the layout? Not fast. A dealer winging cards into your face? Fast! What the hell?

I jerked backward and felt metal in my back. A monstrously large, steroidally enhanced security guard held a gun at my back. I turned to the beautiful AP, who was as wide-eyed as I. What the hell, were we going to be shot in the fearless owner's casino because we might beat him out of a few bucks? (I knew nothing at that time about various beatings of card counters, not only by this casino but others in Vegas. I was still somewhat of a babe in the woods—a babe in the woods with a gun in my back!)

"Let's just walk right out the front door," I whispered in AP's ear. "Take the chips. The guy isn't going to shoot us with all these people around...I hope."

So we picked up our chips, ignoring the dealer—who had a slight smile on his face—and not even looking at all the people eyeballing us. We didn't even acknowledge the Incredible Hulk security guard, who I guessed was foaming and growling, and we headed for the door through the crowds at the craps tables—crowds I was praying the Incredible Hulk would not shoot into. I mean, why kill regular players? How badly could a regular player hurt a fearless casino?

Leaving that way, I doubted the Incredible Hulk would try to plug us with all those players around. Still, my heart was beating 4,000 beats a minute. Thankfully, we weren't shot. The next day we came back on another shift and cashed in our chips. We also sent in some of our friends to cash in some of our chips as well. We obviously never played in that casino again. In almost 20 years, I have not stepped foot inside it. For all I know, that security guard, now bent and withered, is still there waiting for me.

The lesson I learned in that encounter was a simple one: don't believe what the casinos say about themselves. That casino was afraid of skilled players just like all the other ones, despite its public reputation of being unafraid. The casinos are afraid; they are very afraid. Remember that.

Website owner and avid player Alan Mendelson asked me why we didn't call the police. Good question. It didn't even dawn on us to call the police. We always thought of the police and the casino industry as one and the same. It never crossed our minds to call them.

Although it might seem as if I have had many experiences with barrings, bannings, and trespassing for blackjack, in a quarter century of play, they have not happened all that often. Naturally, when they do happen, they tend to be memorable. AP and I will never forget our Horseshoe horror.

CHAPTER 13

Tanned, Tortured, and Banned in Las Vegas

L et me now go into a week in Vegas when I was banned from one of my favorite casinos of all time—Bellagio. This was my last banning and started a course of action for me that will change my life. While the main ingredient in this banning brew revolved around craps, and perhaps Pai Gow poker, it is endemic to all my other barrings and bannings and the barrings and bannings of a legion of advantage players. It is not only the latest one, but it is a telling one.

While this banning was not for anything "specific," I figured it came because I had successfully played various games such as blackjack, craps, and Pai Gow poker at Bellagio for too many years. I really don't know if Bellagio had a record of my play with the beautiful AP. If it did, I would like to thank them for keeping me around for so long. But all good things do come to an end. Even a monstrous casino such as Bellagio has its limits, and the thought of losing a few bucks can even send such a place into a fit.

What lessons have I learned from this experience? First, never tell anyone where you play if you know mobs will show up. As I became an increasingly more popular writer, I should have become more circumspect. When I say "never tell anyone," I mean anyone you know, unless they are a part of your team—

swear a blood oath if you have to. Bellagio was a great place for a few of us to play, but then it wasn't when the few became the many became the mob. Not all advantage players, be they blackjack or craps players, comport themselves as gentlemen. (I never got a complaint about any ladies.) Get enough people in a given casino, and the few idiots will dictate how the dealers, floor people, and pit bosses see you. Just think of yourself as a teacher with a class of 30 students in front of you; 28 of them are just great kids, but two of them are total shitheads who delight in disrupting your class and hurling nastiness toward you and some of the other students. When you go home, do you think, *Oh, I have so many nice students in that class; I just love to enter that room and teach them,* or do you think, *I wish I could kill those two bastards* and toss and turn into the night?

Anyone who deals with the public knows that a few creeps can ruin what would otherwise have been a very good day. Thus it started to be with Bellagio. The casino got enough mixed nuts on the weeks I played there to make them associate such nuts with me.

Don't keep going back to the same place over and over again. I tended to obey this and jump from casino to casino during my casino career. But in some casinos and in some venues, I just over-did it—I outstayed my welcome. As Ben Franklin wrote: "Guests, like fish, begin to smell after three days." I guess I began to smell.

Finally, if you notice a change in attitude on the part of the dealers—especially if you notice a change in pit personnel and some new dealers who are nasty or sarcastic (as happened at Bellagio)—the time has come to move on. Playing in a place that knows your name is the opposite of the Cheers song—it is probably better that no one knows your name. In my case, as the years went on, my books, articles, and television appearances made it hard for many casino employees not to know my name. Still, bouncing around and leaving if you get even a whiff of trouble is the way to go. As we always said, "There's no such thing as paranoia."

The First Day: Thursday, June 23

A highly foggy week should start with a highly foggy day, and my June trip to Vegas started just that way. When I awoke and looked out my bedroom window, I saw almost nothing but haze. When I left Kennedy Airport in New York that early morning, the fog was so thick you couldn't see more than 50 feet. We got on the plane at the correct time but waited on the tarmac for 20 to 30 minutes before we could take off. That is recorded as an "on-time" flight, even though we got to Vegas about a half hour late.

On Thursdays we set up the hotel banquet rooms for our dice-control classes. We had 19 teachers, all of whom were elite dice controllers, coming in to teach our students how to beat the casinos at craps. But first we all had to set up the banquet rooms.

That Thursday during setup of the practice room, my partner Dominator was in something of an emotional turmoil, which is usual for him. He wants everything the way he wants it, and that's that. He is something of a perfectionist and gets heated when perfection is not achieved—which it rarely is. You can see this during his long rolls at craps. He gets increasingly angry as the roll progresses, because somewhere deep inside him is the knowledge that his roll will end, as all rolls must end, and so much for the perfection he was experiencing. That pending inevitable end angers him because it destroys perfection. So it goes.

I've seen it at blackjack as well. He just can't stand to lose, even a hand, because it ruins the order of the universe; that order being he should win each and every decision in a gambling game. If I didn't know he was sane, I'd think he was nuts.

Unfortunately, nothing goes entirely as planned when we are putting together such a big event, especially in a new place. Last-minute changes are often greeted with charges from the hotel, which can be annoying but understandable, because the hotel is not there to accommodate us for free.

We were doing our classes at the Alexis Park Resorts, a beautiful non-casino property on Harmon Avenue, across the street from the

Hard Rock. It really is a resort, too with three swimming pools, a restaurant, a gym, with every room a suite—a really nice place.

Setting up our practice room on Thursday is tough work. We have three full craps tables, two half tables, and anywhere from four to eight throwing and receiving stations, depending on the size of the class. The student-teacher ratio, a key to the intense personal instruction we give, is usually four students to two teachers. Each four-student group has a mentor, and each station has an instructor. You are given truly up-close hands-on experience with the best dice controllers in the world.

We used to do Speed Count blackjack classes during those weekends, but with the publishing of *Beat Blackjack Now!: The Easiest Way to Get the Edge!*, the need for such classes totally dried up. Unlike dice control, most blackjack players can learn Speed Count easily in a weekend and actually head right for the casinos to play with an edge. Basic-strategy blackjack players would have no problem learning Speed Count on their own.

As always, there were some small glitches in setting up the various rooms for our weekend. We found that the room where we were to hold the meet-and-greet party on Friday evening was not as air-conditioned as the room next to it that had been set up as the classroom or as cool as the practice room where we had set up our tables. The classroom was cool, the practice room was cool, but the party room was not so cool. We wanted a hot party but in a cool room.

It was too late to change rooms without a fee from the hotel (which annoyed Dominator to no end, so we didn't go that route), and we also didn't want the attendant hassle of doing such a mass moving. So we shut off the lights, opened the doors, and tried to get the air-conditioning from the practice room and the hallway into the party room.

When Thursday's work was finished, my craps team, the Five Horsemen—composed of Dominator, Stickman, Nick@Night, Skinny, and me, along with GTCers Marilyn "the Goddess," Charlie

"Sandtrap," and Arman "Pit Boss"—headed to CraftSteak at MGM Grand for a great meal. The owner of CraftSteak is Chef Tom Colicchio, the leading judge on the reality show *Top Chef*, which the beautiful AP and I love.

I have never had a bad meal at CraftSteak, but something had happened since my last visit the previous June. One of Golden Touch's interns, John "the Rolling Rooster," twice sent me a couple dozen steaks from a new company he had bought and, well, even Mr. Colicchio never tasted steaks that were that good. While I again enjoyed my meal at CraftSteak, I kept thinking that if some cows descended from heaven, the Rolling Rooster's were those cows. Maybe Colicchio should get some of the Rolling Rooster's cows.

The Second Day: Friday, June 24

My normal day at home usually goes something like this: I wake up, do some work—usually answering emails—go swimming three mornings a week, box two mornings a week, and work out on the treadmill two mornings a week. I am not slim but in decent enough shape.

However, when I am in Vegas during a class, things radically change and I rarely get to work out while the class is on.

But I wanted that trip to be different; I wanted to do my workouts every day as I do at home. So Stickman and I decided on Friday morning to get up really early and head to the gym to use their treadmills. But only one of them actually worked, which caused Stickman to volunteer to use the Stairmaster—a torturous device, especially if you have never used one. After that, we'd go to the pool, where I could swim laps.

After the treadmill and "stair slaughter" of Stickman (who always gets the bad end of the stick) we headed for the pool. Of course, early in the morning there were no lifeguards, but I went in anyway. After 13 minutes a really large gun-toting security guard stood at the edge of the pool. Obviously I couldn't ignore him.

"Oh, please don't tell me that I have to get out," I said.

"You have to get out," he said. "The lifeguard doesn't come until 9:30. It's only a little after 7:00."

"I never refuse a man with a gun," I said and slowly made my way out of the pool.

Stickman prefers to lounge and get some sun, and he had one hell of a tan. He uses no tanning lotion, and it amazes me that he never burns. Satan would have a hard time frying him in hell…if there were a hell.

We were expecting in excess of 70 people to attend the meet and greet that night—although some wound up not coming due to airline delays. We had 62; add in 20 instructors, and it was a decent crowd.

Friday evening's meet and greet is tough—tough on me, that is. My audience has heard that I am funny, and many have seen me do "my thing" before, so I do feel pressure to be just that as I introduce our instructors, mentors, and students. The problem is that I can't prepare myself for humor; it comes or it doesn't come. I ad lib my way through my entire stint on stage and hope for the best. So far so good, but I do know that one night—one horrible night—I will bomb and know that my humor days are over. That night has not yet come, but like a seven-out it surely will. If I were Dominator I would be getting angry in advance.

I gave out an award to Charlie "Sandtrap," one of our first two students (his wife Marilyn "the Goddess" was the other) for his blistering 90-roll hand, the fifth-longest hand we have ever recorded, at the Golden Nugget in Atlantic City.

Except for occasional dustups when Dominator got really angry by something someone did that he didn't like—usually someone from the resort—Friday went smoothly. I was (thank you, Lord!) funny, the students and guests at the meet and greet had a great party, and we looked forward to two days of teaching novice (Primers) and intermediate players (Refreshers) the secrets to unlocking their potential to beat the house using dice control and proper betting.

The Third Day: Saturday, June 25

Stickman and I were too tired to get up early and work out. There went mimicking being at home.

Teaching students from 8:00 AM to 5:00 PM is not an easy thing. By the end of the day, the instructors are exhausted, as are the students. The scariest part of the day is when the instructors demonstrate their own controlled throws. I mean, here we are—live and in person—actually doing what we tell them they can learn to do. There is no guarantee that our throws will look good, and we know that our reputations as dice controllers are on the line when we do our demonstrations. So far, after 10 years, we haven't bombed once!

Early that morning I gave a lesson on Speed Count to two of our students who expressed an interest in learning how to get the edge in blackjack. It is always good to have two (or three) advantage games to play, as you often can't get your spot at the craps table or you have become too fatigued to shoot. Card counting is a great alternative to dice control.

The fun break of the classroom day was lunch with the students. In a relaxed atmosphere we can really get to know them and they can get to know us.

Saturday evening, Dominator, Stickman, Skinny, Nick@Night, the Goddess, Sandtrap, Pit Boss, Dice Pilot, his lovely wife, Lilly, and I had dinner at my favorite Italian restaurant, Fiamma, at MGM Grand.

As we entered MGM Grand, we were greeted by a horde of young "ladies" heading out to the Electric Daisy Carnival, a dance marathon at the Las Vegas Speedway that started at 8:00 PM and went until dawn. None of our party was easily shocked, but these young ladies shocked the hell out of us. Many were either in their underwear or almost naked. One was wearing only a bra and a G-string! All of us agreed that we would be completely depressed if any of our daughters turned out that way.

And then Fiamma was the major disappointment. It had been a restaurant with the best homemade pasta I had ever eaten. My mouth would water just thinking about eating there, but it wasn't to be that night. The new chef had created pasta dishes that sounded lackluster—one of which had mint flavor! You can't feed Italian appetites (such as Dominator's) mint-flavored pasta; it is a mortal sin.

Dominator decided to take the bull by the horns, and he requested some meals like we used to have at Fiamma. The chef attempted to make them, but they were a disappointment, except for Stickman's raviolini, which was actually on the new menu.

When the bill came, for the first time ever, Dominator looked at it. We usually just split it up and pay.

"What the hell is this?" he asked nobody in particular.

"What?" I asked him.

"It says 'ice' and 'no ice,' with a charge next to each."

He called the waitress over.

"What's this ice and no ice stuff?" he asked.

"We charge you an extra four dollars if you have ice in your drink," she said.

"Four dollars if I have ice in my drink?"

"Yes," she said.

"And the no ice thing?"

"We charge you two dollars if you don't have ice with your drink because we use ice to chill the glass," she said.

Ten adults, all of whom eat regularly at gourmet restaurants, sat stunned. Charging *for* ice? Charging for *not* ice?

"Check the bill," I murmured. "See if there's a charge for air."

The Fourth Day: Sunday, June 26

If students get a good night's sleep and do not hit the casinos hard on Saturday night, muscle memory begins setting in while they sleep, and on Sunday their throws are much improved. Of course, many students do not listen to our advice about not going berserk that Saturday night, and they come into class somewhat tired or even hungover on Sunday morning. Just looking at such individuals tells you clearly they will probably never become advantage players, because they have no discipline over themselves, much less over how they will play the game.

My two blackjack students had played for about an hour at one of the better casinos for blackjack, and both won some money. They were happy to discover how easy Speed Count was, and they wanted to know if winning consistently was in the offing. That is a mistake we all make at the beginning of our card-counting careers. That is, if that first session is successful, we think we'll just keep winning and winning. I wish it were so. "No, I'm sorry," I said. "You will have ups and downs just like any other gambler. The difference will be that over time you will be up, but getting there is not easy. The pattern is always up and down." (Or down and up.)

On Sunday, the big event is our tournament, where each student gets to compete to see who will become the individual champion and each team competes to see which team will carry home the laurels.

When it was over, we broke down the tables, boxed all the products, took inventory, and went our separate ways. The Five Horsemen, along with the Goddess and Sandtrap, headed for our favorite casino, Bellagio.

At the VIP check-in, I said to Dominator, Skinny, and Nick@Night that my hostess never seemed to get my reservations right. I once showed up and the reservation was listed for the following week; I once showed up, and there were only two days on my reservation instead of four; I once showed up, and there was no reservation. I wondered if our hostess had just put me aside in her mind because this "getting everything wrong" was becoming a refrain.

"You know," I joked, "if I write that fact, no one would believe me. How could Bellagio get an RFB player's reservation wrong time and time again?"

"They'll get it right," said Nick@Night. "She got all of ours right."

I made my way to the desk. "Hi," I said. "Frank Scoblete." I handed her my license and credit card.

She fiddled with the computer. "I'm sorry, you were supposed to come in last night, but you called and cancelled your reservation."

"I never called to cancel anything. Also my reservation is for tonight, Sunday, leaving on Thursday. Please call my hostess and straighten this out if you can. Thanks."

After some 10 minutes on the phone, she smiled and looked up from her computer. "Okay, we have you in tonight, leaving on Tuesday."

"No, no," I said. "I'm leaving on Thursday."

She made another endless phone call. "I'm sorry; yes, you're right. You are RFB, leaving on Thursday. I am sorry about that."

"Don't worry about it. It's not your fault."

I didn't know it at the time, but that was a foreshadowing of worse to come. When things start to go bad they are like vortexes—everything gets sucked up in them, mixes together, and comes out bad. Could it be that the foggy takeoff from Kennedy, the problems Dom had with Alexis Park, the fact that I had better steaks at home than at CraftSteak, that Fiamma had been a major disappointment charging us for ice and no ice, and that my reservation had been totally screwed up by my hostess at Bellagio were all of a piece? Would it be an ongoing piece?

There had been a time in the past when Bellagio was our own private casino. No students or other players knew we played there. Indeed, long before Golden Touch existed, the beautiful AP and I played blackjack at Bellagio, which is where we discovered that the fat-fingered dealers tended to give away their hole cards in faceup games.

The Five Horsemen played there for several years, and even though the dealers and pit crews knew us, there had never been a hassle. Indeed, one pit boss came over to me a few years ago to tell me he had read my books and was a big fan. It was heaven on earth. Indeed, part of why we were liked was that we played the game properly and one of us would tip on every roll of the dice. We're a friendly bunch.

But it slowly got out that after the classes, Bellagio was the place to be, and by that trip easily 50 to 100 players swarmed the place at any given time—even in the wee hours of the morning, because it was known that the Five Horsemen liked to play between 5:00 AM and 6:00 AM. I didn't see such mobs as a big bad deal for the casino because most of the players were not dice controllers, although some of our students could actually beat the house. Still, many of their spouses threw money away on the slot machines. I always figured it was a win-win situation for the casino.

It became a lose-lose situation for us.

Actually, let me change that. It was more of a lose-lose situation for Dominator and Nick@Night, the two Horsemen who were the most anxious to play immediately after class. After 25 years of casino play, I am never in a rush to get to the tables. I also space out my play. I almost never play at night when the tables are crowded, and so Sunday after class is simply a time to relax, have a nice dinner, and get some rest for the next three days of play.

As we walked to the tram that would take us to the Union Restaurant at Aria, the tables at Bellagio were packed with GTCers and those who show up whenever we are at Bellagio.

Our original reservations at Union had been for 8:00 PM, but we changed them to 6:00 PM because we had arrived at Bellagio early. Union said it would be difficult to change the reservations, but Skinny finally got them to do so. I guess on a Sunday night that place must be packed. But Skinny is a master at negotiations, and he got our reservations changed. Skinny's philosophy is that most situations can be resolved with intelligent discussion.

We arrived at Union and...*there was no one there!* Okay, one table had two diners, but the rest of the restaurant was 100 percent completely empty.

"Please wait while we find you a table," said the hostess.

So we went to the bar, which was also empty, and waited a half hour for the hostess to find us a table. I wondered if they were having an invisible-man convention and we just couldn't see all the people eating, albeit silently, in the place. I was beginning to get an eerie feeling that I had been somehow transported to Tunica, Mississippi, where no one ever got anything right.

Finally, several months after Armageddon, we were seated. Evidently, the waitstaff had not yet arrived, or they were hiding somewhere, and so we waited some more. Maybe that's why they are called the "waitstaff"—their job is to make you wait. If so, they did their job extremely well.

When the waiters showed up, they were not the best, but the food was excellent. It was a long meal, because the waiters seemed to vanish into thin air for long periods of time, and the place did start to get some customers by the time we left. There were at least three more tables brimming with hungry people. As far as I know, they might still be there waiting for their meals.

I went back to Bellagio, where at least four tables were packed with GTCers, then up to my bed for some comforting sleep.

The Fifth Day: Monday, June 27

Monday morning, Stickman and I got up early and headed down to the craps tables. I enjoy playing in the early hours—5:00 AM, 6:00 AM—when the tables are usually empty. They were not empty that morning; they were packed.

Stickman and I ambled over to the Pai Gow poker tables. Pai Gow poker is a game that can be beaten because, played properly, you can get a small edge over the house (see *Everything Casino Poker: Get the Edge at Video Poker, Texas Hold'em, Omaha Hi-Lo, and Pai Gow Poker!*).

We played a little, then Dominator, Skinny, and Nick showed up, and we met the Goddess and Sandtrap for breakfast.

And then began the horror for me.

An hour after breakfast, Stickman and I decided to go to the spa and work out. Then we'd head for the pool, where I would swim and Stickman would challenge the sun to do its worst to him.

My stomach was feeling a little weird while I walked on the treadmill. I had earphones on and I was watching the news. *Gurgle, gurgle.* Maybe I was working out too soon after breakfast?

After the workout, we headed for the pool. Bellagio has several pools, all of them lovely, plus Jacuzzis. The big pool was just too crowded to do any laps, and I was feeling kind of bloated anyway. My stomach was still gurgling.

Stickman was sunning himself. I lay down on the recliner next to him and covered myself up. I am not a big fan of sitting in the sun.

I was just feeling a little "off," you might say.

I had taken a nap that afternoon, but I just didn't feel too good. I went down to play some Pai Gow poker, but after two minutes, I knew I was going to get sick. I told Stickman I had to go back to my room. In my room, I realized there was no way I would be able to go to dinner, so I called Stickman and told him to let the others know I was not going out that night.

I slept a couple hours then got up. I was feeling really bloated, as if someone had pumped air bubbles into my belly. I did not feel nauseous—how could I? I hadn't eaten anything since breakfast, and that was 12 hours before.

But that night was awful. Every half hour or so, I would run to the bathroom, thinking I was going to be sick from one end or the other, but each time it was a false alarm, because there was nothing in my stomach to come out.

That went on for 12 hours or so. It was a miserable night. I would have had more fun waiting at Union for a table, a drink, or a meal. I would have had more fun waiting for my reservation for my room to be worked out.

Things calmed down by 6:00 AM on Tuesday.

The Sixth Day: Tuesday, June 28

By 7:00 AM, I was kind of hungry. I ordered room service—a banana and an English muffin.

I went down to play craps, but the tables were again full. I played a little Pai Gow poker, but I was really exhausted. I told my fellow Horsemen I would be missing dinner again that night, went to sleep at 2:00 in the afternoon and woke up on...

The Last Playing Day: Wednesday, June 29

At 5:00 AM.

I had slept 15 straight hours, but even though I felt a little weak, I knew I was better. I took a hot shower and just let the water warm me and relax me. I called Stickman and also left a message for Dominator and Skinny that I was feeling okay and that I'd be down to play craps at about 6:30.

When I met Stickman and Skinny downstairs, the craps tables still had too many people at them, and our preferred spots were not available. As a dice controller, you have several spots where you can successfully shoot. If those spots are not open, it is best not to play.

We didn't play.

We went over to the Pai Gow poker tables and took one that was empty. Stickman, Skinny, and I bought in, and several minutes later Not2Soon tooled over, and we convinced him to play.

"My reputation will be ruined if I play this game," he laughed. But he cashed in, too.

When we play we all like to bank (when our friends bank we don't play against them), and when we bank after any other players have played their hands, we enjoy putting the cards on the table one at a time. This really increases the suspense of the game, kind of like a slot machine showing one symbol at a time—delightful suspense. But that morning, the floor person would not let us do it—something we had been doing for more than four years.

And then came this:

From nowhere it seemed, *he* appeared and immediately got right in my face. "We've all read your books and we know what you're doing. We don't like it. We don't want you here!" He made a kind of wave to cover what looked like the whole casino.

This guy was new to me; he was an "upstairs suit" and he came from on high with his loud clarion call broadcasting to everyone near me that it would be best if I left his property and went elsewhere.

"I wouldn't give you any comp time if you hadn't taken out a marker," he snarled. "Why don't you go across the street to Caesars? They'd love your action. You're rich. You can play anywhere."

I'm rich? I can play anywhere?

The upstairs suit then added, "One of your guys roughed up one of our pit people last night at the craps table. We have it on tape."

One of my guys? My guys? I don't have any guys.

The masses of GTCers who played at Bellagio were responsible for themselves. Really, would one of our former students actually "rough up" a pit boss?

I know that weekend and during that week one student had an 85 roll, and there were several 50+-roll hands and many 30+-roll hands. Could the GTCers have actually hit this massive casino hard enough to make the bosses sweat? I couldn't see that at all, no matter how hot some of our players had gotten. Just 50 feet from us at that very moment in time was a player on a reserved table betting $50,000 a number! I didn't see any sweat flying off any casino bosses' heads because of that!

The boss screaming in my face could be unnerving to some players. I felt nothing. I looked at him as I looked at the false fronts and silly themes of an industry geared to fooling people into giving away their money on games that they couldn't beat. Maybe that gun in my back long before had made me appreciate even an angry, seemingly apoplectic casino suit.

Skinny was red-faced. He had never been through something like that at a casino. Skinny is a man of reason, but he was being confronted with loathing directed at me. I looked at Stickman;

he was staring at the raving executive. At 6'4", Stickman can be scary when he stares. He's a big man. I looked at Not2Soon, and he seemed to be calm and relaxed. He'd been through it in his own playing career before. I really think he was only worried that people would think he would actually play Pai Gow poker.

Though this had happened to me before, I never liked it. I don't do anything illegal, and I merely try to help players win or cut the house edge down as much as possible—something that is wrong in the eyes of the casino bosses. Had my books, tapes, television appearances, and classes really hurt Bellagio? Had the Five Horsemen crippled the casino with our play? Were all those GTCers flooding the tables with all the hangers-on really doing any monumental harm to Bellagio's bottom line? I doubted it.

Were some players winning over a long period of time? Yes. They were true advantage players of the first order. Were most of the GTC followers who charged into the casino to play with the dice-control elite winning scads of money over time? No. Watching the way those players wagered was a sure indication that they were just your typical losers. They also played for endless hours, even after all the real dice controllers had long gone to bed.

But none of that mattered to the suit spewing at me. When a casino boss gets it into his head that you are no longer welcome at his casino, then that is, as they say, that.

"Could you show me the tape? I'd love to see who roughed up the pit person," I said.

"I am not going to do anything about that," he said. "I really don't want you here. I don't like what you do. I know what you're trying to do."

"Okay," I said.

"I would leave if I were you," he said. "I'm being obnoxious to you. Do you really want to try to play here? Look how I'm treating you. I want you out of here. Do you understand?"

"I understand how you feel," I said. "You aren't being obnoxious; you're just doing what you feel you need to do."

There was a long pause. I think the executive thought I was going to yell back at him or be nasty or sarcastic and then he could have me escorted out or arrested. That would have been Dom, not me. Dom has been in a number of confrontations that the casino always won because he was on their property. There is never a point in arguing a barring or a banning. The casino suit was the boss. He had a perfect right to tell me he didn't like my books, my playing, my students, or me. He could even tell someone who had done nothing illegal that he wasn't welcome in a place; the law had given him that right. Yes, it is the "wrongest right" in the casino world, but it is the right the casinos have.

He immediately cooled down. He was no longer angry.

"You understand?" he asked.

"I understand," I said.

He walked away. We colored up.

"Well, that's it for Bellagio," I said.

"Yes," Stickman said.

"No," said the eminently reasonable Skinny, "there has to be some way to straighten this out. He didn't officially ban you, did he?"

"Yes," I said. "He did. That's what you call a nice banning. He told me to get out. Had we continued to play, he would have made it official."

"That was a nice banning," Not2Soon agreed.

Dominator and Nick@Night arrived a few moments later.

We told them our tale. Dominator and I had indeed noticed in the past year or so that the Bellagio pit crews and some dealers were not quite as friendly as they had been in the past. Actually quite a few of the individuals were new to us. Many of Bellagio's pit personnel and dealers had moved to other casinos, especially Aria, which was next door. When I had played at Aria a couple of times, the dealers and floor people were exceedingly friendly—in fact, I knew almost all of them from my past play at Bellagio.

Dominator had noticed that when he played at Bellagio some of the new dealers were starting to make cracks about him and his shooting. Dom is not one to take things lightly, as you now know, and so he would fire back at them. It wasn't helpful. He went to our hostess a couple of times to complain as well. None of that worked. The hostess was the type of woman who really didn't seem to care, and besides, she had no power over the games, the crews of the games, or the casino suits in charge of the games. When you play properly (as we do), when you tip all the time (as we do), if you still get sarcastic remarks and snickers, you aren't going to change anyone's mind by complaining or snickering or being sarcastic back to them.

It took Skinny about 12 hours of trying to figure out how to fix our banning before he finally realized it was over. No talk, no intelligent discussion, no anything would change the mind of the suit who represented the casino that didn't want our action.

Dominator and Nick@Night went home soon after, and Stick-man, Skinny, Not2Soon, and I planned our day. We went over to Mandalay Bay to see the Shark Reef exhibit, a great underwater world of fishes and turtles, and then Not2Soon headed home.

That night we celebrated my birthday, then Stickman headed for the airport, and Skinny and I went to see *Viva Elvis*—a show I really enjoyed that had gotten mixed reviews from some of my friends. It has since closed.

After the show, heading back to Bellagio, Skinny was still trying to assimilate what had happened that day.

"I just can't believe it," he said. "I just can't believe it."

The next morning the limo (yes, Bellagio still honored my RFB) took me to the airport. I looked out the back window as the limo was pulling away from the property. Bellagio came into full view and then started to get smaller.

"Good-bye, Bellagio," I said in a whisper. "Good-bye."

Appendix I

Card-Counting Methods

Blackjack can be beaten. That is a simple, unassailable fact. Given a decent amount of penetration, just about every game can give the player the edge if the player does four things:

1. Knows the basic strategy for the game

2. Knows a legitimate card-counting system

3. Raises the bet when the remaining cards favor the player

4. Lowers the bet when the remaining cards favor the house

When the dealer finishes the shuffle, she will put a plastic card, called the "cut card," into the deck or shoe, cutting some cards behind it out of play. This card is usually yellow. How many cards she cuts off decides whether there is good, average, or poor penetration.

There are many card-counting systems that go from the extremely difficult to learn to the traditional one-level systems such as Hi-Lo to the easiest system ever developed, known as Speed Count.

There have been many misunderstood and downright wrong card-counting concepts floated out to the general public by casinos and popular literature and film, the first of which is that card counting is against the law. Not so. It is perfectly legal. There are no laws that state you must stop using your brain in a casino.

While it does seem that many people do stop using their brains in casinos, doing so is a matter of choice and not some mandate of the gods or nature or the state legislatures, whose members are also voted in by people who seem to have forsaken their brains at the voting booth.

Some movies, such as *Rain Man*, make it sound as if a card counter has to have a mind like Albert Einstein's in order to keep track of every card in the deck or shoe. That is nonsense. Traditional card counting is simply adding, subtracting, and dividing small numbers—and remembering the total results from round to round.

There will be counts where the casino has the edge, and there will be counts where the player has the edge. Anyone with normal intelligence can do this; no genius-level IQ or savant abilities such as Rain Man's are required.

There is also the myth that card counting only works in single-deck or double-deck games and that four-, six-, and eight-deck games are immune to it. Again the movie *Rain Man* pushes this false idea when a scene shows two security personnel in the control room saying (and I paraphrase): "He can't be counting because no one can count into six decks!" Maybe the movie producers had to add that line to the script in order to be allowed to film in the casino. No matter; the movie is fiction, as is the false statement made by those actors playing security agents.

There are many card-counting systems, and I will take a look at three: the traditional Hi-Lo system, Paul Keen's system, and the amazingly simple Speed Count system.

A. THE HI-LO SYSTEM

The Hi-Lo system, which is fully explained in my book *Beat Blackjack Now!: The Easiest Way to Get the Edge!*, tracks the 2s, 3s, 4s, 5s, and 6s, along with the 10-valued cards and aces, giving them plus or minus points as they come out of the deck or shoe.

Plus Cards	Neutral Cards	Minus Cards
2 = +1	7 = 0	10 = –1
3 = +1	8 = 0	Jack = –1
4 = +1	9 = 0	Queen = –1
5 = +1		King = –1
6 = +1		Ace = –1

There are 20 plus cards and 20 minus cards. The count is at zero when the game begins. When more plus cards come out of the deck or shoe, the count will become favorable to the player. When more minus cards come out of the deck or shoe, the count will be unfavorable for the player. Naturally, having a deck that favors the player does not mean the player must automatically win the next hand. It simply means that the player is statistically more likely to make money over time with the deck or shoe containing more high cards.

When the count is at a certain plus level, then the player will start to make bigger bets to take advantage of his edge. When the count is in a neutral or minus level, the player will make smaller bets.

Since the casino starts off with an edge at the beginning of the game, even though the count is zero, the game will still favor the house in small plus counts. The plus count has to get to different levels depending on the game for the player to have a real mathematical advantage over the house.

So why do the large cards remaining in a deck or shoe favor the player and the small cards favor the casino? Large cards make a blackjack more likely, and although players and dealers will get the same percentage of blackjacks, the players are paid 3-to-2. The reverse is also true. With more small cards remaining, the likelihood of a blackjack is less—and that favors the house.

Even though in positive counts the dealer will get to stand more often, he is also more apt to bust his 16-and-lower hands since there are more high cards in the shoe waiting to come out, and the dealer must hit any hand that is 16 or less. However, with more small cards remaining, when he hits those 16-or-lower hands, he has a better chance of not busting.

Card counting using the traditional Hi-Lo system has you add the positive cards (2, 3, 4, 5. and 6) when they come out of the deck or shoe and subtract the negative cards (10, jack, queen, king, and ace) when they are dealt. The 7, 8, and 9 are neutral cards and are ignored.

When the deck or shoe is at zero, what is the count when the following cards come out?

Player One: ace/10
Player Two: 5/6/7
Player Three: 7/4/6
Dealer: 8/2/5/3

Player One brings the count down to minus two (–2) as both the ace and 10 are negative ones. Player Two brings the count up to zero again because 5 and 6 are each a plus one while 7 is neutral. Player Three brings the count to plus two (+2), because the 7 is neutral but the 4 and 6 are plus ones. With the dealer's 8 (neutral), 2 (+1), 5 (+1), and 3 (+1), the count is +5. It is positive.

Is this positive count of +5 enough to give the player the edge over the casino, or is it just not enough? Let's see.

The +5 count above is called the "running count" and indicates the number of plus and minus cards that have come out of the deck. However, to understand whether you have an edge or not, the player must bring into play his skills at division in order to arrive at the "true count." It is the true count that tells a player whether he has an edge, how large that edge is, and what he should bet into that edge.

Let's take a look at multiple-deck shoe games first.

The true count is arrived at by dividing the number of remaining decks to be played into the running count. So if five decks remain to be played in the shoe, with a running count of +5, the true count is a +1. What if the true count results in a fraction such as +2.6? In that case you always drop the fraction and use +2 as the true count; if it is a –2.6, you round the fraction and make the true count –3. These are safety measures you should follow.

Since many shoes cover the cards so the players cannot see them, arriving at the true count requires the player to look at the discard pile to determine as best he can how many decks have already been played. You subtract the decks played from the number of decks in the game to arrive at your figure. So if you are playing a six-deck game and two decks have come out, four decks remain. You divide these four decks into your running count to get your true count.

Although the math is relatively simple in Hi-Lo, probably the simplest of the traditional counts, it can still be difficult doing this in a casino because of all the constant distractions. It takes time to master, and you shouldn't expect to become proficient without a lot of practice in and out of the casinos. Patience will, however, pay off, and after a while doing the count in the casino will be second nature...well, for some players, that is.

Single-deck games (with a 3-to-2 payout for blackjacks) are a different story.

Arriving at the true count for single-deck games will always require you to deal with fractions. That can be a tortuous, head-spinning procedure. Instead, you can use the running count for single-deck games without too much worry about not being accurate. In single-deck games the true-count conversion of the running count is just not that important, especially for a relatively new player.

So what would that running count of +5 be in a single-deck game? It would be a monster plus count because the impact of a single card in a single-deck game is far stronger than the impact of a single card in a multiple-deck game.

In single-deck games with decent rules, you can use the following betting scheme:

Single Deck				
Count	Units	$10 Player	$25 Player	$100 Player
0 or less	1	$10	$25	$100
+1	2	$20	$50	$200
+2	3	$30	$75	$300
+3	4	$40	$100	$400
+4	4 or 5	$40 or $50	$100 or $125	$400 or $500
+5	4 or 5	$40 or $50	$100 or $125	$400 or $500
+6 or more	4 or 5	$40 or $50	$100 or $125	$400 or $500

The single-deck chart goes as high as five units, but the more you increase your bet in jumps, the better the chance the casino floor person or pit boss will wonder why you are doing so. Increasing your bet does not have to be done in whole numbers as shown above. You could go to two units on +1, and when the count jumps to +4, just go to three units, and if you win the hand, even if the count goes down to +2, you can then increase your hand to four units or 3.5 units, etc. Playing around with your bets in high counts can at times reduce your edge somewhat, but it can also allow you to stay at the tables for longer periods of time.

Double Deck				
True Count	Units	$10 Player	$25 Player	$100 Player
0 or less	1	$10	$25	$100
+1	1	$10	$25	$100
+2	2	$20	$50	$200
+3	4	$40	$100	$400
+4	6	$60	$150	$600
+5	8	$80	$200	$800
+6 or more	8 to 10	$80 to $90 to $100	$200 to $225 to $250	$800 to $900 to $1,000

Four Decks				
True Count	*Units*	*$10 Player*	*$25 Player*	*$100 Player*
0 or less	1	$10	$25	$100
+1	1	$10	$25	$100
+2	2	$20	$50	$200
+3	4	$40	$100	$400
+4	8	$80	$200	$800
+5	8	$80	$200	$800
+6 or more	8 to 10	$80 to $90 to $100	$200 to $225 to $250	$800 to $900 to $1,000

Six Decks				
True Count	*Units*	*$10 Player*	*$25 Player*	*$100 Player*
0 or less	1	$10	$25	$100
+1	1	$10	$25	$100
+2	2	$20	$50	$200
+3	4	$40	$100	$400
+4	6	$60	$150	$600
+5	12	$120	$300	$1,200
+6 or more	12 to 14	$120 to $130 to $140	$300 to $325 to $350	$1,200 $1,300 to $1,400

Eight Decks				
True Count	*Units*	*$10 Player*	*$25 Player*	*$100 Player*
0 or less	1	$10	$25	$100
+1	1	$10	$25	$100
+2	2	$20	$50	$200
+3	4	$40	$100	$400
+4	6	$60	$150	$600
+5	12	$120	$300	$1,200
+6 or more	12 to 14	$120 to $130 to $140	$300 to $325 to $350	$1,200 $1,300 to $1,400

As I stated, you do not have to increase your bets by whole numbers. You can change your betting scheme around each and every time you decide to increase your bet. These charts are really

for reference—albeit a strong reference—but you do not have to
be a slave to them.

Using Basic Strategy

What follows are the basic strategies for the various numbers of decks
and rules you'll encounter. You'll note that there is very little difference between these strategies and you could simply take the first
one for each grouping (4-6-8 decks, 2 decks, 1 deck) and simply use
that one. The difference in your winning expectation will be changed
only by a fraction, should you do this. You can make a handy card
to bring to the table as well because just about all casinos allow you
to look up the right decisions as far as hitting, standing, splitting,
doubling, and so forth.

4-6-8 decks; dealer STANDS on 17; double after splits

S=stand; H=hit; D=double down; P=split; U=surrender

For boxes with a slash (/), use play on the left if permitted; if not, use play on the right.

Hand	2	3	4	5	6	7	8	9	10	Ace
8	H	H	H	H	H	H	H	H	H	H
9	H	D/H	D/H	D/H	D/H	H	H	H	H	H
10	D/H	D/H	D/H	D/H	D/H	D/H	D/H	D/H	H	H
11	D/H	D/H	D/H	D/H	D/H	D/H	D/H	D/H	D/H	H
12	H	H	S	S	S	H	H	H	H	H
13	S	S	S	S	S	H	H	H	H	H
14	S	S	S	S	S	H	H	H	H	H
15	S	S	S	S	S	H	H	H	U/H	H
16	S	S	S	S	S	H	H	U/H	U/H	U/H
17	S	S	S	S	S	S	S	S	S	S
A-2	H	H	H	D/H	D/H	H	H	H	H	H
A-3	H	H	H	D/H	D/H	H	H	H	H	H
A-4	H	H	D/H	D/H	D/H	H	H	H	H	H
A-5	H	H	D/H	D/H	D/H	H	H	H	H	H
A-6	H	D/H	D/H	D/H	D/H	H	H	H	H	H
A-7	H	D/S	D/S	D/S	D/S	S	S	H	H	H
A-8	S	S	S	S	S	S	S	S	S	S
A-9	S	S	S	S	S	S	S	S	S	S
A-A	P	P	P	P	P	P	P	P	P	P
2-2	P	P	P	P	P	P	H	H	H	H
3-3	P	P	P	P	P	P	H	H	H	H
4-4	H	H	H	P	P	H	H	H	H	H
5-5	D/H	D/H	D/H	D/H	D/H	D/H	D/H	D/H	H	H
6-6	P	P	P	P	P	H	H	H	H	H
7-7	P	P	P	P	P	P	H	H	H	H
8-8	P	P	P	P	P	P	P	P	P	P
9-9	P	P	P	P	P	S	P	P	S	S
10-10	S	S	S	S	S	S	S	S	S	S

4-6-8 decks; dealer STANDS on 17; no double after splits

S=stand; H=hit; D=double down; P=split; U=surrender

For boxes with a slash (/), use play on the left if permitted;
if not, use play on the right.

Hand	2	3	4	5	6	7	8	9	10	Ace
8	H	H	H	H	H	H	H	H	H	H
9	H	D/H	D/H	D/H	D/H	H	H	H	H	H
10	D/H	D/H	D/H	D/H	D/H	D/H	D/H	D/H	H	H
11	D/H	D/H	D/H	D/H	D/H	D/H	D/H	D/H	D/H	H
12	H	H	S	S	S	H	H	H	H	H
13	S	S	S	S	S	H	H	H	H	H
14	S	S	S	S	S	H	H	H	H	H
15	S	S	S	S	S	H	H	H	U/H	H
16	S	S	S	S	S	H	H	U/H	U/H	U/H
17	S	S	S	S	S	S	S	S	S	S
A-2	H	H	H	D/H	D/H	H	H	H	H	H
A-3	H	H	H	D/H	D/H	H	H	H	H	H
A-4	H	H	D/H	D/H	D/H	H	H	H	H	H
A-5	H	H	D/H	D/H	D/H	H	H	H	H	H
A-6	H	D/H	D/H	D/H	D/H	H	H	H	H	H
A-7	S	D/S	D/S	D/S	D/S	S	S	H	H	H
A-8	S	S	S	S	S	S	S	S	S	S
A-9	S	S	S	S	S	S	S	S	S	S
A-A	P	P	P	P	P	P	P	P	P	P
2-2	H	H	P	P	P	P	H	H	H	H
3-3	H	H	P	P	P	P	H	H	H	H
4-4	H	H	H	P	P	H	H	H	H	H
5-5	D/H	D/H	D/H	D/H	D/H	D/H	D/H	D/H	H	H
6-6	H	P	P	P	P	H	H	H	H	H
7-7	P	P	P	P	P	P	H	H	H	H
8-8	P	P	P	P	P	P	P	P	P	P
9-9	P	P	P	P	P	S	P	P	S	S
10-10	S	S	S	S	S	S	S	S	S	S

4-6-8 decks; dealer HITS soft 17 (Ace-6); double after splits

S=stand; H=hit; D=double down; P=split; U=surrender

*For boxes with a slash (/), use play on the left if permitted;
if not, use play on the right.*

Hand	2	3	4	5	6	7	8	9	10	Ace
8	H	H	H	H	H	H	H	H	H	H
9	H	D/H	D/H	D/H	D/H	H	H	H	H	H
10	D/H	D/H	D/H	D/H	D/H	D/H	D/H	D/H	H	H
11	D/H	D/H	D/H	D/H	D/H	D/H	D/H	D/H	D/H	D/H
12	H	H	S	S	S	H	H	H	H	H
13	S	S	S	S	S	H	H	H	H	H
14	S	S	S	S	S	H	H	H	H	H
15	S	S	S	S	S	H	H	H	U/H	H
16	S	S	S	S	S	H	H	U/H	U/H	U/H
17	S	S	S	S	S	S	S	S	S	U/S
A-2	H	H	H	D/H	D/H	H	H	H	H	H
A-3	H	H	H	D/H	D/H	H	H	H	H	H
A-4	H	H	D/H	D/H	D/H	H	H	H	H	H
A-5	H	H	D/H	D/H	D/H	H	H	H	H	H
A-6	H	D/H	D/H	D/H	D/H	H	H	H	H	H
A-7	D/S	D/S	D/S	D/S	D/S	S	S	H	H	H
A-8	S	S	S	S	D/S	S	S	S	S	S
A-9	S	S	S	S	S	S	S	S	S	S
A-A	P	P	P	P	P	P	P	P	P	P
2-2	P	P	P	P	P	P	H	H	H	H
3-3	P	P	P	P	P	P	H	H	H	H
4-4	H	H	H	P	P	H	H	H	H	H
5-5	D/H	D/H	D/H	D/H	D/H	D/H	D/H	D/H	H	H
6-6	P	P	P	P	P	H	H	H	H	H
7-7	P	P	P	P	P	P	H	H	H	H
8-8	P	P	P	P	P	P	P	P	P	P
9-9	P	P	P	P	P	S	P	P	S	S
10-10	S	S	S	S	S	S	S	S	S	S

4-6-8 decks; dealer HITS soft 17 (Ace-6); no double after splits

S=stand; H=hit; D=double down; P=split; U=surrender

*For boxes with a slash (/), use play on the left if permitted;
if not, use play on the right.*

Hand	2	3	4	5	6	7	8	9	10	Ace
8	H	H	H	H	H	H	H	H	H	H
9	H	D/H	D/H	D/H	D/H	H	H	H	H	H
10	D/H	D/H	D/H	D/H	D/H	D/H	D/H	D/H	H	H
11	D/H	D/H	D/H	D/H	D/H	D/H	D/H	D/H	D/H	D/H
12	H	H	S	S	S	H	H	H	H	H
13	S	S	S	S	S	H	H	H	H	H
14	S	S	S	S	S	H	H	H	H	H
15	S	S	S	S	S	H	H	H	U/H	H
16	S	S	S	S	S	H	H	U/H	U/H	U/H
17	S	S	S	S	S	S	S	S	S	U/S
A-2	H	H	H	D/H	D/H	H	H	H	H	H
A-3	H	H	H	D/H	D/H	H	H	H	H	H
A-4	H	H	D/H	D/H	D/H	H	H	H	H	H
A-5	H	H	D/H	D/H	D/H	H	H	H	H	H
A-6	H	D/H	D/H	D/H	D/H	H	H	H	H	H
A-7	D/S	D/S	D/S	D/S	D/S	S	S	H	H	H
A-8	S	S	S	S	D/S	S	S	S	S	S
A-9	S	S	S	S	S	S	S	S	S	S
A-A	P	P	P	P	P	P	P	P	P	P
2-2	H	H	P	P	P	P	H	H	H	H
3-3	H	H	P	P	P	P	H	H	H	H
4-4	H	H	H	H	H	H	H	H	H	H
5-5	D/H	D/H	D/H	D/H	D/H	D/H	D/H	D/H	H	H
6-6	H	P	P	P	P	H	H	H	H	H
7-7	P	P	P	P	P	P	H	H	H	H
8-8	P	P	P	P	P	P	P	P	P	P
9-9	P	P	P	P	P	S	P	P	S	S
10-10	S	S	S	S	S	S	S	S	S	S

TWO decks; dealer STANDS on 17; double after splits

S=stand; H=hit; D=double down; P=split; U=surrender

For boxes with a slash (/), use play on the left if permitted; if not, use play on the right.

Hand	2	3	4	5	6	7	8	9	10	Ace
8	H	H	H	H	H	H	H	H	H	H
9	D/H	D/H	D/H	D/H	D/H	H	H	H	H	H
10	D/H	D/H	D/H	D/H	D/H	D/H	D/H	D/H	H	H
11	D/H	D/H	D/H	D/H	D/H	D/H	D/H	D/H	D/H	D/H
12	H	H	S	S	S	H	H	H	H	H
13	S	S	S	S	S	H	H	H	H	H
14	S	S	S	S	S	H	H	H	H	H
15	S	S	S	S	S	H	H	H	U/H	H
16	S	S	S	S	S	H	H	H	U/H	U/H
17	S	S	S	S	S	S	S	S	S	S
A-2	H	H	H	D/H	D/H	H	H	H	H	H
A-3	H	H	H	D/H	D/H	H	H	H	H	H
A-4	H	H	D/H	D/H	D/H	H	H	H	H	H
A-5	H	H	D/H	D/H	D/H	H	H	H	H	H
A-6	H	D/H	D/H	D/H	D/H	H	H	H	H	H
A-7	H	D/S	D/S	D/S	D/S	S	S	H	H	H
A-8	S	S	S	S	S	S	S	S	S	S
A-9	S	S	S	S	S	S	S	S	S	S
A-A	P	P	P	P	P	P	P	P	P	P
2-2	P	P	P	P	P	P	H	H	H	H
3-3	P	P	P	P	P	P	H	H	H	H
4-4	H	H	H	P	P	H	H	H	H	H
5-5	D/H	D/H	D/H	D/H	D/H	D/H	D/H	D/H	H	H
6-6	P	P	P	P	P	P	H	H	H	H
7-7	P	P	P	P	P	P	P/H	H	H	H
8-8	P	P	P	P	P	P	P	P	P	P
9-9	P	P	P	P	P	S	P	P	S	S
10-10	S	S	S	S	S	S	S	S	S	S

TWO decks; dealer STANDS on 17; no double after splits

S=stand; H=hit; D=double down; P=split; U=surrender

For boxes with a slash (/), use play on the left if permitted; if not, use play on the right.

Hand	2	3	4	5	6	7	8	9	10	Ace
8	H	H	H	H	H	H	H	H	H	H
9	D/H	D/H	D/H	D/H	D/H	H	H	H	H	H
10	D/H	D/H	D/H	D/H	D/H	D/H	D/H	D/H	H	H
11	D/H	D/H	D/H	D/H	D/H	D/H	D/H	D/H	D/H	D/H
12	H	H	S	S	S	H	H	H	H	H
13	S	S	S	S	S	H	H	H	H	H
14	S	S	S	S	S	H	H	H	H	H
15	S	S	S	S	S	H	H	H	U/H	H
16	S	S	S	S	S	H	H	H	U/H	U/H
17	S	S	S	S	S	S	S	S	S	S
A-2	H	H	H	D/H	D/H	H	H	H	H	H
A-3	H	H	H	D/H	D/H	H	H	H	H	H
A-4	H	H	D/H	D/H	D/H	H	H	H	H	H
A-5	H	H	D/H	D/H	D/H	H	H	H	H	H
A-6	H	D/H	D/H	D/H	D/H	H	H	H	H	H
A-7	S	D/S	D/S	D/S	D/S	S	S	H	H	H
A-8	S	S	S	S	S	S	S	S	S	S
A-9	S	S	S	S	S	S	S	S	S	S
A-A	P	P	P	P	P	P	P	P	P	P
2-2	H	H	P	P	P	P	H	H	H	H
3-3	H	H	P	P	P	P	H	H	H	H
4-4	H	H	H	H	H	H	H	H	H	H
5-5	D/H	D/H	D/H	D/H	D/H	D/H	D/H	D/H	H	H
6-6	P	P	P	P	P	H	H	H	H	H
7-7	P	P	P	P	P	P	H	H	H	H
8-8	P	P	P	P	P	P	P	P	P	P
9-9	P	P	P	P	P	S	P	P	S	S
10-10	S	S	S	S	S	S	S	S	S	S

TWO decks; dealer HITS soft 17 (Ace-6); double after splits

S=stand; H=hit; D=double down; P=split; U=surrender

For boxes with a slash (/), use play on the left if permitted; if not, use play on the right.

Hand	2	3	4	5	6	7	8	9	10	Ace
8	H	H	H	H	H	H	H	H	H	H
9	D/H	D/H	D/H	D/H	D/H	H	H	H	H	H
10	D/H	D/H	D/H	D/H	D/H	D/H	D/H	D/H	H	H
11	D/H	D/H	D/H	D/H	D/H	D/H	D/H	D/H	D/H	D/H
12	H	H	S	S	S	H	H	H	H	H
13	S	S	S	S	S	H	H	H	H	H
14	S	S	S	S	S	H	H	H	H	H
15	S	S	S	S	S	H	H	H	U/H	U/H
16	S	S	S	S	S	H	H	H	U/H	U/H
17	S	S	S	S	S	S	S	S	S	U/S
A-2	H	H	H	D/H	D/H	H	H	H	H	H
A-3	H	H	D/H	D/H	D/H	H	H	H	H	H
A-4	H	H	D/H	D/H	D/H	H	H	H	H	H
A-5	H	H	D/H	D/H	D/H	H	H	H	H	H
A-6	H	D/H	D/H	D/H	D/H	H	H	H	H	H
A-7	D/S	D/S	D/S	D/S	D/S	S	S	H	H	H
A-8	S	S	S	S	D/S	S	S	S	S	S
A-9	S	S	S	S	S	S	S	S	S	S
A-A	P	P	P	P	P	P	P	P	P	P
2-2	P	P	P	P	P	P	H	H	H	H
3-3	P	P	P	P	P	P	H	H	H	H
4-4	H	H	H	P	P	H	H	H	H	H
5-5	D/H	D/H	D/H	D/H	D/H	D/H	D/H	D/H	H	H
6-6	P	P	P	P	P	P	H	H	H	H
7-7	P	P	P	P	P	P	P	H	H	H
8-8	P	P	P	P	P	P	P	P	P	P
9-9	P	P	P	P	P	S	P	P	S	S
10-10	S	S	S	S	S	S	S	S	S	S

TWO decks; dealer HITS soft 17 (Ace-6); no double after splits

S=stand; H=hit; D=double down; P=split; U=surrender

For boxes with a slash (/), use play on the left if permitted;
if not, use play on the right.

Hand	2	3	4	5	6	7	8	9	10	Ace
8	H	H	H	H	H	H	H	H	H	H
9	D/H	D/H	D/H	D/H	D/H	H	H	H	H	H
10	D/H	D/H	D/H	D/H	D/H	D/H	D/H	D/H	H	H
11	D/H	D/H	D/H	D/H	D/H	D/H	D/H	D/H	D/H	D/H
12	H	H	S	S	S	H	H	H	H	H
13	S	S	S	S	S	H	H	H	H	H
14	S	S	S	S	S	H	H	H	H	H
15	S	S	S	S	S	H	H	H	U/H	U/H
16	S	S	S	S	S	H	H	H	U/H	U/H
17	S	S	S	S	S	S	S	S	S	U/S
A-2	H	H	H	D/H	D/H	H	H	H	H	H
A-3	H	H	D/H	D/H	D/H	H	H	H	H	H
A-4	H	H	D/H	D/H	D/H	H	H	H	H	H
A-5	H	H	D/H	D/H	D/H	H	H	H	H	H
A-6	H	D/H	D/H	D/H	D/H	H	H	H	H	H
A-7	D/S	D/S	D/S	D/S	D/S	S	S	H	H	H
A-8	S	S	S	S	D/S	S	S	S	S	S
A-9	S	S	S	S	S	S	S	S	S	S
A-A	P	P	P	P	P	P	P	P	P	P
2-2	H	H	P	P	P	P	H	H	H	H
3-3	H	H	P	P	P	P	H	H	H	H
4-4	H	H	H	H	H	H	H	H	H	H
5-5	D/H	D/H	D/H	D/H	D/H	D/H	D/H	D/H	H	H
6-6	P	P	P	P	P	H	H	H	H	H
7-7	P	P	P	P	P	P	H	H	H	H
8-8	P	P	P	P	P	P	P	P	P	P
9-9	P	P	P	P	P	S	P	P	S	S
10-10	S	S	S	S	S	S	S	S	S	S

SINGLE deck; dealer STANDS on 17; double after splits

S=stand; H=hit; D=double down; P=split; U=surrender

For boxes with a slash (/), use play on the left if permitted;
if not, use play on the right.

Hand	2	3	4	5	6	7	8	9	10	Ace
8	H	H	H	D/H	D/H	H	H	H	H	H
9	D/H	D/H	D/H	D/H	D/H	H	H	H	H	H
10	D/H	D/H	D/H	D/H	D/H	D/H	D/H	D/H	H	H
11	D/H	D/H	D/H	D/H	D/H	D/H	D/H	D/H	D/H	D/H
12	H	H	S	S	S	H	H	H	H	H
13	S	S	S	S	S	H	H	H	H	H
14	S	S	S	S	S	H	H	H	H	H
15	S	S	S	S	S	H	H	H	H	H
16	S	S	S	S	S	H	H	H	U/H	U/H
17	S	S	S	S	S	S	S	S	S	S
A-2	H	H	D/H	D/H	D/H	H	H	H	H	H
A-3	H	H	D/H	D/H	D/H	H	H	H	H	H
A-4	H	H	D/H	D/H	D/H	H	H	H	H	H
A-5	H	H	D/H	D/H	D/H	H	H	H	H	H
A-6	D/H	D/H	D/H	D/H	D/H	H	H	H	H	H
A-7	S	D/S	D/S	D/S	D/S	S	S	H	H	S
A-8	S	S	S	S	D/S	S	S	S	S	S
A-9	S	S	S	S	S	S	S	S	S	S
A-A	P	P	P	P	P	P	P	P	P	P
2-2	P	P	P	P	P	P	H	H	H	H
3-3	P	P	P	P	P	P	P	H	H	H
4-4	H	H	P	P	P	H	H	H	H	H
5-5	D/H	D/H	D/H	D/H	D/H	D/H	D/H	D/H	H	H
6-6	P	P	P	P	P	P	H	H	H	H
7-7	P	P	P	P	P	P	P	H	U/S	H
8-8	P	P	P	P	P	P	P	P	P	P
9-9	P	P	P	P	P	S	P	P	S	S
10-10	S	S	S	S	S	S	S	S	S	S

SINGLE deck; HIT soft 17 (Ace-6); no double after splits

S=stand; H=hit; D=double down; P=split; U=surrender

For boxes with a slash (/), use play on the left if permitted; if not, use play on the right.

Hand	2	3	4	5	6	7	8	9	10	Ace
8	H	H	H	D/H	D/H	H	H	H	H	H
9	D/H	D/H	D/H	D/H	D/H	H	H	H	H	H
10	D/H	D/H	D/H	D/H	D/H	D/H	D/H	D/H	H	H
11	D/H	D/H	D/H	D/H	D/H	D/H	D/H	D/H	D/H	D/H
12	H	H	S	S	S	H	H	H	H	H
13	S	S	S	S	S	H	H	H	H	H
14	S	S	S	S	S	H	H	H	H	H
15	S	S	S	S	S	H	H	H	U/H	H
16	S	S	S	S	S	H	H	H	U/H	U/H
17	S	S	S	S	S	S	S	S	S	U/S
A-2	H	H	D/H	D/H	D/H	H	H	H	H	H
A-3	H	H	D/H	D/H	D/H	H	H	H	H	H
A-4	H	H	D/H	D/H	D/H	H	H	H	H	H
A-5	H	H	D/H	D/H	D/H	H	H	H	H	H
A-6	D/H	D/H	D/H	D/H	D/H	H	H	H	H	H
A-7	S	D/S	D/S	D/S	D/S	S	S	H	H	S
A-8	S	S	S	S	D/S	S	S	S	S	S
A-9	S	S	S	S	S	S	S	S	S	S
A-A	P	P	P	P	P	P	P	P	P	P
2-2	H	P	P	P	P	P	H	H	H	H
3-3	H	H	P	P	P	P	H	H	H	H
4-4	H	H	H	D/H	D/H	H	H	H	H	H
5-5	D/H	D/H	D/H	D/H	D/H	D/H	D/H	D/H	H	H
6-6	P	P	P	P	P	H	H	H	H	H
7-7	P	P	P	P	P	P	H	H	U/S	U/H
8-8	P	P	P	P	P	P	P	P	P	P
9-9	P	P	P	P	P	S	P	P	S	S
10-10	S	S	S	S	S	S	S	S	S	S

SINGLE deck; STAND on 17; no double after splits
S=stand; H=hit; D=double down; P=split; U=surrender
For boxes with a slash (/), use play on the left
if permitted; if not, use play on the right.

Hand	2	3	4	5	6	7	8	9	10	Ace
8	H	H	H	D/H	D/H	H	H	H	H	H
9	D/H	D/H	D/H	D/H	D/H	H	H	H	H	H
10	D/H	D/H	D/H	D/H	D/H	D/H	D/H	D/H	H	H
11	D/H	D/H	D/H	D/H	D/H	D/H	D/H	D/H	D/H	D/H
12	H	H	S	S	S	H	H	H	H	H
13	S	S	S	S	S	H	H	H	H	H
14	S	S	S	S	S	H	H	H	H	H
15	S	S	S	S	S	H	H	H	H	H
16	S	S	S	S	S	H	H	H	U/H	U/S
17	S	S	S	S	S	S	S	S	S	S
A-2	H	H	D/H	D/H	D/H	H	H	H	H	H
A-3	H	H	D/H	D/H	D/H	H	H	H	H	H
A-4	H	H	D/H	D/H	D/H	H	H	H	H	H
A-5	H	H	D/H	D/H	D/H	H	H	H	H	H
A-6	D/H	D/H	D/H	D/H	D/H	H	H	H	H	H
A-7	S	D/S	D/S	D/S	D/S	S	S	H	H	S
A-8	S	S	S	S	D/S	S	S	S	S	S
A-9	S	S	S	S	S	S	S	S	S	S
A-A	P	P	P	P	P	P	P	P	P	P
2-2	H	P	P	P	P	P	H	H	H	H
3-3	H	H	P	P	P	P	H	H	H	H
4-4	H	H	H	D/H	D/H	H	H	H	H	H
5-5	D/H	D/H	D/H	D/H	D/H	D/H	D/H	D/H	H	H
6-6	P	P	P	P	P	H	H	H	H	H
7-7	P	P	P	P	P	P	H	H	U/S	H
8-8	P	P	P	P	P	P	P	P	P	P
9-9	P	P	P	P	P	S	P	P	S	S
10-10	S	S	S	S	S	S	S	S	S	S

B. DAN PRONOVOST'S SPEED COUNT

Speed Count was developed by blackjack mathematician and computer expert Dan Pronovost over a three-year period. It is fully presented in my book *Beat Blackjack Now!: The Easiest Way to Get the Edge!*

On average the player and the dealer will receive 2.7 cards per hand, one being a small card, so you add up the small cards that have come out (2, 3, 4, 5, and 6) and you subtract the number of completed hands (including the dealer's hand) from the total.

You *do not* add or subtract while the cards are being dealt. You are not interested in the cards; you are interested in *the hands*, and hands only matter when the player *stops playing* his cards.

And what is the total that you subtract these numbers from, since you aren't adding and subtracting +1 or –1 from each other as you do in the traditional Hi-Lo count?

Okay, let us take a typical two-deck game first.

Dan Pronovost has determined through computer simulations that the count for a double-deck game starts at 30. Oh, and forget everything you just read about Hi-Lo, because you have now entered the brave new and wonderful world of Speed Count.

Let us say there are two players and the dealer. That's *three hands* being played. So you will subtract 3 from the total after a round. If there is a split, you will subtract four hands. If there are two splits, you will subtract five hands. Splits count as separate hands. Are splits a big deal? Not really, they occur about 2 percent of the time.

The dealer deals out the cards. You get a 10 and a 2, the other player gets a 6 and 4, and the dealer shows a 6 as the up-card. So do you start counting right then? No. Why? Because no hand has been played.

Traditional card counters are busily counting high cards and low cards and adding and dividing right then, but you are doing nothing. You do not count a small card until *a hand has been played*, even hands swept off the board by a dealer's blackjack.

What makes Speed Count unique is the fact that you are adding small cards and subtracting them based on *the number of hands*, and if a hand is not finished, there is no counting.

Okay, let's do a round:

You stand on your 10 and 2 against the dealer's 6. Your hand is finished. The count is 31—you started with 30 on the two-deck game, added one for your small card of 2, and so you have a 31 count.

Then it's the other player's turn. He doubles on his 6 and 4 and gets a 5. His hand is finished. There are three small cards added to your 31 (6, 4, and 5), and the Speed Count is at 34.

The dealer turns over the hole card, a 10, and she has 16. She hits and busts with a 10. You add her small card (the 6) to the total of 34, and you have 35.

Three hands were played, so you subtract 3 from 35 and get 32. That is your count, 32, which means a real mathematical edge over the house. Counts of 31 and over show a positive expectation for the player in every blackjack game!

You started the two-deck game at the count of 30. When a hand was completed, you added all the small cards to your starting number of 30. We went to 35 at the end of the round. You then subtracted the number of hands from the total to arrive at your new count. We subtracted three hands from 35 to arrive at 32.

And that is Speed Count. Easy as can be!

Of course, not all games are two-deck games. While the player will have the edge every time the count is at 31 in every game, the starting number for Speed Count will change based on the number of decks. Here's how to begin your Speed Count with various decks:

Number of Decks	Speed Count Begins at:	Edge Begins at:
Single deck	30	31
Double deck	30	31
Four decks	29	31
Six decks	27	31
Eight decks	26	31

The rules of the game and the penetration of the game will determine how strong your edge is at 31—but 31 will always mean an edge at all games. If the casino allows DAS, S17, resplits, and surrender, your 31 will be stronger than a 31 in a game where the dealer hits soft 17 (H17), where you can't double after splits, and where you can't resplit or surrender. As the count goes up to 32, 33, 34, 35, and higher, your edge over the casino gets stronger.

At 30, the casino has an edge in all games. As the count goes down to 29, 28, 27, 26, 25, etc., the house edge over you becomes stronger.

Speed Count Betting Ranges

Single Deck: Count starts at 30				
Speed Count	*Units*	*$10 Player*	*$25 Player*	*$100 Player*
27 or lower	Exit game	Exit game	Exit game	Exit game
30 or lower	1	$10	$25	$100
31	2	$20	$50	$200
32	3	$30	$75	$300
33	4	$40	$100	$400
34 or higher	5	$50	$125	$500
33 or higher	Insure hand	Insure hand	Insure hand	Insure hand

Double Deck: Count starts at 30				
Speed Count	*Units*	*$10 Player*	*$25 Player*	*$100 Player*
26 or lower	Exit game	Exit game	Exit game	Exit game
30 or lower	1	$10	$25	$100
31	2	$20	$50	$200
32	4	$40	$100	$400
33	5	$50	$125	$500
34 or higher	6	$60	$150	$600
34 or higher	Insure hand	Insure hand	Insure hand	Insure hand

Four Decks: Count starts at 29				
Speed Count	*Units*	*$10 Player*	*$25 Player*	*$100 Player*
23 or lower	Exit game	Exit game	Exit game	Exit game
30 or lower	1	$10	$25	$100
31	2	$20	$50	$200
32	3	$30	$75	$300
33	4	$40	$100	$400
34	5	$50	$125	$500
35	6	$60	$150	$600
36 or higher	7	$70	$175	$700
37 or higher	Insure hand	Insure hand	Insure hand	Insure hand

Six Decks: Counts starts at 27				
Speed Count	*Units*	*$10 Player*	*$25 Player*	*$100 Player*
21 or lower	Exit game	Exit game	Exit game	Exit game
30 or lower	1	$10	$25	$100
31	2	$20	$50	$200
32	4	$40	$100	$400
33 and above	8	$80	$200	$800
38 or higher	Insure hand	Insure hand	Insure hand	Insure hand

Eight Decks: Count starts at 26				
Speed Count	*Units*	*$10 Player*	*$25 Player*	*$100 Player*
20 or lower	Exit game	Exit game	Exit game	Exit game
30 or lower	1	$10	$25	$100
31	2	$20	$50	$200
32	4	$40	$100	$400
33	6	$60	$150	$600
34	8	$80	$200	$800
35 and above	10	$100	$250	$1000
40 or higher	Insure hand	Insure hand	Insure hand	Insure hand

There you have it, the simplest card-counting system ever developed that can give the player a decent edge. Is Speed Count as powerful as the Hi-Lo count? No, it isn't, but again a player will tend to make more mistakes at Hi-Lo than at Speed Count, so it can often be a wash between the two. Obviously, if you are a successful Hi-Lo counter, there would be no reason to switch to Speed Count. However, basic-strategy players should seriously consider an upgrade in their game when it comes to Speed Count.

Speed Count has its own unique basic strategy called OBS—Optimum Basic Strategy. This strategy makes the Speed Count more powerful, and you should use it.

Here is a generic Optimum Basic Strategy for Speed Count:

Generic Optimum Basic Strategy
S=stand; H=hit; D=double down; P=split; U=surrender

**Game is 2-4-6-8 decks; dealer HITS on soft 17 (ace-6);
double after splits allowed**
*For boxes with a slash (/), use play on the left if permitted;
if not, use play on the right.*

Hand	2	3	4	5	6	7	8	9	10	Ace
8	H	H	H	H	*D/H	H	H	H	H	H
9	*D/H	D/H	D/H	D/H	D/H	H	H	H	H	H
10	D/H	D/H	D/H	D/H	D/H	D/H	D/H	D/H	H	H
11	D/H	D/H	D/H	D/H	D/H	D/H	D/H	D/H	D/H	*D/H
12	H	*S	S	S	S	H	H	H	H	H
13	S	S	S	S	S	H	H	H	H	H
14	S	S	S	S	S	H	H	H	H	H
15	S	S	S	S	S	H	H	H	U/H	*U/H
16	S	S	S	S	S	H	H	U/H	*U/S	U/H
17	S	S	S	S	S	S	S	S	S	S
A-2	H	H	H	D/H	D/H	H	H	H	H	H
A-3	H	H	*D/H	D/H	D/H	H	H	H	H	H
A-4	H	H	D/H	D/H	D/H	H	H	H	H	H
A-5	H	H	D/H	D/H	D/H	H	H	H	H	H
A-6	H	D/H	D/H	D/H	D/H	H	H	H	H	H
A-7	*D/S	D/S	D/S	D/S	D/S	S	S	H	H	H
A-8	S	S	S	S	*D/S	S	S	S	S	S
A-9	S	S	S	S	S	S	S	S	S	S
A-A	P	P	P	P	P	P	P	P	P	P
2-2	P	P	P	P	P	P	H	H	H	H
3-3	P	P	P	P	P	P	H	H	H	H
4-4	H	H	H	P	P	H	H	H	H	H
5-5	D/H	D/H	D/H	D/H	D/H	D/H	D/H	D/H	H	H
6-6	P	P	P	P	P	H	H	H	H	H
7-7	P	P	P	P	P	P	*P	H	*U/H	*U/H
8-8	P	P	P	P	P	P	P	P	*U/P	*U/P
9-9	P	P	P	P	P	S	P	P	S	S
10-10	S	S	S	S	S	S	S	S	S	S

C. PAUL KEEN'S SYSTEM

Paul Keen's system is the system presented in the book *Blackjack Your Way to Riches* by Richard Canfield. It was called "the expert system." It is similar to the Hi-Lo but with some interesting substitutions. The system took away the 2 and ace in the count—these became neutral cards—and added the 7 as a plus card and the 9 as a minus card. So the count system looks this way:

Card	Value
King	−1
Queen	−1
Jack	−1
10	−1
9	−1
Ace	0
2	0
8	0
3	+1
4	+1
5	+1
6	+1
7	+1

You would use the same basic strategies that you use for Hi-Lo and the same betting spread, using the running count and the true count in shoe games. You do not have to use these in single-deck games. You can ramp up your betting just as you do with the Hi-Lo.

The Hi-Lo is a superior system, but Keen's system is not bad. Given a choice, you obviously go with the better system, which is Hi-Lo.

Appendix II

Books and Resources

There is far more information on Hi-Lo, Speed Count, and other areas of blackjack in my book *Beat Blackjack Now!: The Easiest Way to Get the Edge!* The book is available on my website (www. frankscoblete.com), on Amazon, from your local bookstore, and from my mail-order company at 1-800-944-0406. You can also send a check or money order for $22.95 (that includes the postage) to Frank Scoblete Enterprises, PO Box 446, Malverne, NY 11565.

The book lays out methods for increasing one's edge even as a basic-strategy player. It gives you all levels of the new "optimum" basic strategy that can only be used with Speed Count to increase its power over the casino. There are detailed bankroll recommendations as well, based on a concept called "risk of ruin." You'll also find excellent information about tournament blackjack and Spanish 21.

If you are looking to really hammer the casinos at blackjack, this is the book to read.

My website is www.frankscoblete.com.

My Facebook page is www.facebook.com/frankscoblete.

All my books are on my website under "Scobe's Products" or on Amazon, in major bookstores, or by calling 1-800-944-0406. You can find out more about me under "About Frank Scoblete" on my website.

STANFORD WONG

Stanford Wong has contributed as much to blackjack knowledge as anyone in the field. I highly recommend his *Professional Blackjack* book as an ongoing resource. Wong's website is www.BJ21.com. Wong also has a newsletter called *Current Blackjack News*.

Basic Blackjack
Betting Cheap Claimers
Blackjack Secrets
Casino Tournament Strategy
Optimal Strategy for Pai Gow Poker
Professional Video Poker
Sharp Sports Betting
Winning Without Counting
Wong on Dice

Wong's Software
BJEdge
Blackjack Count Analyzer
Tournament Blackjack
Video Poker Analyzer

DAN PRONOVOST
Dan Pronovost has created excellent software programs that I highly recommend:

For Basic Strategy: Blackjack Mentor
http://www.deepnettech.com/blackjack.html#mentor

For Hi-Lo: Professional Bundle
http://www.deepnettech.com/bjbundles.html#professional

For Speed Count: Speed Count Bundle
http://www.deepnettech.com/bjbundles.html#speedcount

All Bundles:
http://www.deepnettech.com/bjbundles.html#bundles

HENRY TAMBURIN
Blackjack: Take the Money and Run
Craps: Take the Money and Run
Legends of Blackjack

Winning Baccarat Strategies

Another excellent resource for blackjack players is Henry Tamburin's monthly email newsletter *Blackjack Insider*, featuring the top blackjack writers in the country. Henry's website is www.bjinsider. com. All of Henry Tamburin's books are available on his website at http://www.smartgaming.com/.

MORE BLACKJACK BOOKS OF INTEREST

Beat the Dealer by Edward O. Thorp
The Big Book of Blackjack by Arnold Snyder
Blackbelt in Blackjack by Arnold Snyder
Blackjack: Play Like the Pros by John Bukofsky
Blackjack: The Real Deal by J. Phillip Vogel
Blackjack Attack by Don Schlesinger
Blackjack Bluebook II by Fred Renzey
Blackjack Blueprint: How to Play Like a Pro...Part-Time by
    Rick Blaine
Blackjack for Blood by Bryce Carlson
The Blackjack Life by Nathaniel Tilton
The Blackjack Zone by Eliot Jacobson, PhD
Blackjack Your Way to Riches by Richard Canfield
Get the Edge at Blackjack by John May
Ken Uston on Blackjack by Ken Uston and Roy Hoppe
Knock-Out Blackjack by Olaf Vancura and Ken Fuchs
Million Dollar Blackjack by Ken Uston
Modern Blackjack Second Edition Volume I by Norm
    Wattenberger
Modern Blackjack Second Edition Volume II by Norm
    Wattenberger
One-Third of a Shoe by Ken Uston
Play Blackjack Like the Pros by Kevin Blackwood
Playing Blackjack as a Business by Lawrence Revere
The Pro's Guide to Spanish 21 and Australian Pontoon by
    Katarina Walker

Radical Blackjack by Arnold Snyder

The Smarter Bet Guide to Blackjack by Basil Nestor

The Theory of Blackjack by Peter A. Griffin

Two Books on Blackjack by Ken Uston

The World's Greatest Blackjack Book by Lance Humble

PERSONAL BLACKJACK STORIES

1536 Free Waters and Other Blackjack Endeavors by Glen Wiggy

The Big Player by Ken Uston, with Roger Rapoport and Roy Hoppe

Blackjack Autumn by Barry Meadow

Bringing Down the House by Ben Mezrich

Burning the Tables in Las Vegas by Ian Andersen

The Counter by Kevin Blackwood

Repeat Until Rich by Josh Axelrad

The Ultimate Edge by Mark Billings

Frank Scoblete's Hilarious New Book!

Bless me father for I have sinned.

Confessions of a Wayward Catholic

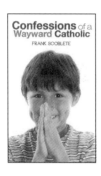

Confessions of a Wayward Catholic is a hilarious yet insightful account of Frank Scoblete's years from kindergarten through grandparenthood as a confused, wayward, seemingly ever-sinning Catholic. Join Frank for an entertaining but possibly hell-bound ride as he attempts to understand what God and religion are all about. Will Frank reach the pearly gates or be banished to eternal damnation?

"I love my husband, but there is stuff in this book that is disgraceful and should never have been written!"
— *Alene Scoblete, wife*

"Francis Scoblete has been a major sinner ever since he came to elementary school. I watched him closely at the dances."
— *Sister Jerome Blake, in charge of making sure girls and boys slow danced a foot apart*

"I don't know why Jewish kids went to a Catholic school, but I'm proud they did well in religion."
— *Chief Rabbi Sol Bernstein*

"I believe that you should love your neighbor as yourself. Luckily, Frank lives in another town and is not my neighbor."
— *Jesus Christ*

"Scoblete says I have no sense of humor. I will afflict him with boils and sores over his whole body, just like I did Job."
— *God*

"Frank Scoblete has been wayward for more than six decades. He's my main man!"
— *Satan*

About the Author

F rank Scoblete is the best-selling author of 30 books and several television shows. He writes for more than 40 magazines and newspapers. Frank is the leading authority on casino games. He has appeared on CNN, TBS, History Channel, A&E, Travel Channel, National Geographic Channel, and the Learning Channel.

Find Frank on the web at www.frankscoblete.com.

Visit his Facebook page at www.facebook.com/frankscoblete.

Available in paperback and as an e-book on Amazon.com and other Internet sites.

Also available from FSE Publishing: Price $16.95 plus $6 shipping and handling.

Call 1-800-944-0406 or send check or money order to Frank Scoblete Enterprises, PO Box 446, Malverne, NY 11565.

The Canon of Frank Scoblete

Armada Strategies for Spanish 21 [Bonus Books]

Baccarat Battle Book [Bonus Books, Taylor Trade Publishing]

Beat Blackjack Now!: The Easiest Way to Get the Edge! [Triumph Books]

Beat the Craps Out of the Casinos: How to Play Craps and Win! [Bonus Books, collectors' item only]

Beat the Craps Out of the Casinos: How to Play Craps and Win! (expanded edition) [Bonus Books, collector's item only]

Best Blackjack [Bonus Books, Taylor Trade Publishing]

Best Blackjack (expanded edition) [Bonus Books]

Bold Card Play!: Best Strategies for Caribbean Stud, Let It Ride & Three Card Poker [Bonus Books]

Break the One-Armed Bandits: How to Come Out Ahead When You Play the Slots [Bonus Books, out of print]

The Captain's Craps Revolution [Paone Press, collector's edition only]

The Captain's Special Report: How to Win at Tournament Craps [Paone Press, out of print]

Casino Conquest: Beat the Casinos at Their Own Games! [Triumph Books]

Casino Craps: Shoot to Win! (with DVD) [Triumph Books]

Casino Gambling: Play Like a Pro in 10 Minutes or Less! [Bonus Books, Taylor Trade Publishing]

Confessions of a Wayward Catholic [FSE Publishing]

The Craps Underground: The Inside Story of How Dice Controllers Are Winning Millions from the Casinos [Bonus Books, Taylor Trade Publishing]

Cutting Edge Craps: Advanced Strategies for Serious Players [Triumph Books]

Everything Casino Poker: Get the Edge at Video Poker, Texas Hold'em, Omaha Hi-Lo, and Pai Gow Poker [Triumph Books]

Forever Craps: The Five-Step Advantage-Play Method [Bonus Books, Taylor Trade Publishing]

Golden Touch Blackjack Revolution! [Research Services Unlimited, out of print]

Golden Touch Dice Control Revolution! [Research Services Unlimited, out of print]

Guerrilla Gambling: How to Beat the Casinos at Their Own Games! [Bonus Books, Taylor Trade Publishing]

Guerrilla Gambling: How to Beat the Casinos at Their Own Games! (updated edition) [Bonus Books, Taylor Trade Publishing]

I am a Dice Controller: Inside the World of Advantage-Play Craps! [Triumph Books, winter 2015]

The Morons of Blackjack and Other Monsters! (as King Scobe) [Paone Press]

Slots Conquest: How to Beat the Slot Machines! [Triumph Books]

Spin Roulette Gold: Secrets of Beating the Wheel [Bonus Books, Taylor Trade Publishing]

Trev: A Novel [FSE Publishing, winter 2015]

Victory at Video Poker [Bonus Books, outdated]

The Virgin Kiss and Other Stories [Research Services Unlimited]

Frank Contributed Chapters or Forewords to

109 Ways to Beat the Casinos, edited by Walter Thomason [Bonus Books]

American Casino Guide, edited by Steve Bourie [Casino Vacations Press]

Blackjack for the Clueless by Walter Thomason [Lyle Stuart]

The Casino Answer Book by John Grochowski [Taylor Trade Publishing]

The Experts' Guide to Casino Games, edited by Walter Thomason [Lyle Stuart]

Gambler's Digest, edited by Dennis Thornton [Krause Publications]

Twenty-First Century Blackjack by Walter Thomason [Bonus Books]

Frank Scoblete's Videotapes, Hosted by James Coburn

Winning Strategies: Blackjack [outdated format]

Winning Strategies: Craps [outdated format]

Winning Strategies: Slots with Video Poker [outdated format]

Frank Scoblete's DVDs

Breaking Vegas: Dice Dominator [History Channel]

Golden Touch: Beat Craps by Controlling the Dice written and hosted by Frank Scoblete [Golden Touch Publishing]

Special Online Series with Video Jug [http://www.videojug.com/interview/gambling-basics-2]

Frank Scoblete's Audio Tapes

Power of Positive Playing! [outdated format]

Sharpshooter Craps! [outdated format]

Slot Conquest! [outdated format]

Frank Scoblete's *Get The Edge* Guides

77 Ways to Get the Edge at Casino Poker by Fred Renzey [Bonus Books, Taylor Trade Publishing]

Get the Edge at Blackjack: Revolutionary Advantage Play Methods That Work! by John May [Bonus Books]

Get the Edge at Craps by Chris Pawlicki (as Sharpshooter) [Bonus Books]

Get the Edge at Low-Limit Texas Hold'em by Bill Burton [Bonus Books, Taylor Trade Publishing]

Get the Edge at Roulette: How to Predict Where the Ball Will Land! by Christopher Pawlicki [Bonus Books, Taylor Trade Publishing]

How to Win Millions Playing Slot Machines...or Lose Trying by Frank Legato [Bonus Books, Taylor Trade Publishing]

Insider's Guide to Internet Gambling by John G. Brokopp [Bonus Books, out of print]

The Lottery Book: The Truth Behind the Numbers by Don Catlin [Bonus Books, Taylor Trade Publishing]

Thrifty Gambling by John G. Brokopp [Bonus Books]

Produced Plays

Dracula's Blind Date

The Virgin Kiss

Frank's books are available at bookstores and on Amazon.com. Many are available in e-book editions for Kindle and other e-readers. You can also purchase them by calling 1-800-944-0406.